We Called It
The Home

We Called It *The* Home

Vignettes and Memories from my 13 Years
in the Ohio Soldiers' and Sailors' Orphans' Home

Janice Daulbaugh Steele-Gouch

ORANGE *frazer* PRESS
Wilmington, Ohio

Published for the author by:
Orange Frazer Press
P.O. Box 214
Wilmington, OH 45177
Telephone: 937.382.3196
For price and shipping information.
Website: www.orangefrazer.com

Book and cover design: Kelly Schutte and Orange Frazer Press

Library of Congress Control Number: 2019939402

First Printing

Dedicated with much love and respect to my older brother Rick and my big sister Jeannie who led our way on this adventure.

A special dedication to the memory of my brother, Jerry, who left us way too soon. We shared so much of this journey together, and this is his story, too.

Also dedicated to all the other children who passed through the Home gates. While this is my story, much of it is their story, too.

And lastly to my children and grandchildren. I hope you will enjoy a glimpse into my childhood.

Acknowledgments

This book would not have been possible without invaluable assistance from several friends.

Thanks to Karen and Lauri for all your editing patience, assistance and encouragement. I couldn't have written this book without your help.

Thanks to Darlene, Dave, Joysan, Will, and James for allowing me to pick your brains as we recalled memories. Thanks to Kathy Trnka Camarena and James Koski for allowing me to share your poems about the Home, more great memories with which I certainly identify.

Thanks to my friends from my Guided Autobiography Group for your encouragement to keep writing.

To my hubby, Jim, special thanks for putting up with me and keeping our lives on track while I was busy writing. And thanks for reading these pages over and over, always offering encouraging suggestions.

Table of Contents

Foreword

In Tribute to Ohio's Veterans

The evening arrived; the boys took their places. The Master, in his cook's uniform, stationed himself at the copper; his pauper assistants ranged themselves behind him; the gruel was served out; and a long grace was said over the short commons. The gruel disappeared; the boys whispered to each other, and winked at Oliver; while his next neighbors nudged him. Child as he was, he was desperate with hunger, and reckless with misery. He rose from the table; and advancing to the master, basin and spoon in hand, said: somewhat alarmed at his own temerity:

"Please, sir, I want some more."

The master was a fat, healthy man; but he turned very pale. He gazed in stupefied astonishment on the small rebel for some seconds, and then clung for support to the copper. The assistants were paralyzed with wonder; the boys with fear.

"What!" said the master at length, in a faint voice.

"Please, sir," replied Oliver, "I want some more."

The master aimed a blow at Oliver's head with the ladle; pinioned him in his arm; and shrieked aloud for the beadle.

The board were sitting in solemn conclave, when Mr. Bumble rushed into the room in great excitement, and addressing the gentleman in the high chair, said,

"Mr. Limbkins, I beg your pardon, sir! Oliver Twist has asked for more!"

There was a general start. Horror was depicted on every countenance.

"For MORE!" said Mr. Limbkins. "Compose yourself, Bumble, and answer me distinctly. Do I understand that he asked for more, after he had eaten the supper allotted by the dietary?"

"He did, sir," replied Bumble.

"That boy will be hung," said the gentleman in the white waistcoat. "I know that boy will be hung."

—From *Oliver Twist* by Charles Dickens, pub. 1838

It is amazing what a piece of literature can do to the community mind at just the right time in history. Dickens wrote this to draw attention to the inhumane treatment of the poor, the orphaned, and the destitute in Victorian England. *Oliver Twist* was published in England only twenty-seven years before the terrible War Between the States ended on this continent. Immediately the orphans of that war began appearing on the streets and in the poor houses of America. People here had read Dickens. And these were American children! No one with a heart could allow this situation to continue.

Many solutions were tried throughout the country with varying degrees of success. Orphanages were one of the most logical ways to care for these innocent victims of the war. The State of Ohio, at the urging of many groups including the clergy and most notably the veterans, created the Ohio Soldiers' and Sailors' Orphans' Home (OSSO Home) on a hillside farm above Xenia, Ohio. Forest was pulled down to begin building what would become an extraordinary experiment in housing, educating, training, and loving children. There have been many orphanages in the United States. Some have had great success. Some, sadly, perhaps came closer to the horrors portrayed by Dickens. But very few gave the wonderful childhood to the children who lived there as did "The Home" on that hill in Ohio.

War followed war in our history. The War of 1812 left new orphans in Ohio who made their way to Xenia, followed by needy orphans of The Spanish American War, The First World War, The Second World War, The Korean Conflict and Vietnam. From 1870 when the OSSO Home opened, there was always a place for our Ohio servicemen's children in desperate need to find a home. I do not imply it was a perfect place. It was a home and a school, made up of and led by humans. But it must have been bathed in much prayer because, of the thousands of children who passed through the Home gates, the vast majority remember it with love and gratitude. So many were and are successful citizens. Many gave their lives for their country. Many, many returned to help the Home after they graduated.

I believe the reason this children's home was exemplary from the very beginning of its existence was Ohio's veterans. In The Civil War, Ohio had the largest loss of life in the North. Even President Lincoln said, "Ohio has saved the union!" But the cost! All those fatherless children! The veterans of the Grand Old Army formed a powerful lobby and as long as they lived, the

OSSO Home was their priority. Whether the governor and state legislature was Democratic or Republican, each politician knew he needed the backing of these veterans. So the Home received funding to be established and to grow. In the eyes of the veterans, the state was not paying charity to these children. They were paying part of a debt to the fathers of these children who had given, in many cases, all for their country. So the children were never treated as paupers but as part of a great and well-loved family. There would be no Oliver Twists at the Home!

This held true generation after generation. The veterans' values never changed, and they and their ladies never deserted the orphans. In time, the Grand Old Army faded away and various new veterans' groups formed, but in Ohio, that meant looking out for the OSSO Home and the children.

In my first reading of Janice Daulbaugh Gouch's compelling memoir of her years in the Home, her time there seemed too good to be true to me. I understood being away from her extended family was difficult for her and her siblings. But all-in-all, it seemed like she had had just too good of a life. After all, she was in an orphanage!

Reading more of the Home's history and Ohio's history, I began to see that for the 130 years of this extraordinary place's existence, people—the veterans, the politicians, the administrators, the clergy, the staff, the faculty, and the families who placed their children at the Home—did some really good things with and for children! They went beyond politics and acted out of wisdom and love. It is a great story. Janice's part of the greater story, told here, is a window into man coming close to acting as man should act.

—*Laurel Ann Fritz Williams*

Introduction

"Orphans–Not what we were, but who we were; a badge of honor."
–James Koski, A Fellow Orphan

The Ohio Soldiers' and Sailors' Orphans' Home was my home from August 14, 1956, mere days before I started kindergarten, until June 1, 1969, my high school graduation day. We all just called it "the Home."

Situated on almost 500 acres in Xenia, Ohio, it was home to over 13,500 children who passed through its gates. Some children, like me, were "lifers" who spent their entire childhood and adolescence as residents of this institution. Others were there for shorter periods of time. Some children were there one day and gone the next. Very seldom did we know when friends were leaving. Rather, they were suddenly just gone, and we never heard from most of them again.

The Home was created during Ohio Governor Rutherford B. Hayes' administration as a home for orphans of Ohio veterans from the Civil War. Over time, admission requirements were changed to accept children of veterans from subsequent wars, and eventually to any child of an Ohio veteran. The Home accepted its first child in 1869, and its last child departed in 1995. In 1978, when admission requirements were relaxed even more in order to admit any needy child in Ohio, the name of the Home was changed to the Ohio Veterans' Children's Home. No matter the name, it was still "the Home" to all these children.

The Home opened with a population of 125 children. Population peaked at about 900 in 1889, with 500 children being the average population over the years.

The Home, funded by the State of Ohio, was governed by a Board of Trustees; five members appointed by the Ohio Governor. It was managed by a superintendent appointed by the Board. The administrative staff reported to the superintendent, who was legal guardian of all the children in the Home.

The campus encompassed more than forty buildings (listed below). In addition to the buildings were beautiful, well-manicured grounds, a parade field, playgrounds, children's cemetery, and football/track stadium.

Armory—Mannington Building
Auditorium—Julian R. Rooney Auditorium, built circa 1936 (Orfrenz Den located in basement)
Band Shell
Cottages—Boys: Adams, Cleveland, Harding, Harrison, Madison, Roosevelt
Cottages—Girls: Garfield, Hayes, Jackson, Jefferson, Monroe, Taft
Cottages—Junior Campus: Taylor and Washington
Cottages—Peter Pan 1–7
Children's Dining Room (CDR)—William T. Amos Hall
Collier Chapel, built in 1873
Employee Residences
Farm
Green House
Gymnasium—McKinley Building, built in 1924
Hobby Shop—AXP Memorial Building
Hospital—Major Warren J. Keifer Building
Industrial Building—Balmer Building
Laundry, Plumbing & Paint Shop Building
Main Building—Grant Hall, built circa 1870
Main Building Annex—Mooney Building
School Buildings (Academic)—Lincoln Building, built circa 1944
School Buildings (Vocational)—James Barnett Building, built in 1931
Storeroom Annex
Superintendent's Residence

To learn more about the Home, *A Home of Their Own: The Story of Ohio's Greatest Orphanage*, written by Edward Lentz and published by Orange Frazer Press, provides a more complete history of this institution.

Prologue

"Everybody needs his memories.
They keep the wolf of insignificance from the door." –Saul Bellow

The traffic light beside the old county courthouse turned red, and I found myself staring up at the familiar brick building. I thought back and clearly remembered that day. I was five years old, sitting in my family's car, parked outside this very same courthouse. It was over sixty years ago, but the building is the same as in my memory, the deep red bricks, the white trim.

The four of us were waiting impatiently in the car. We'd been sitting a long time—was it minutes? Hours? Our beloved grandma had business in court that day. She was relinquishing custody of me and my three siblings to the State of Ohio.

We had already seen the child psychologist. Each of us must have passed his "putting the square block in the square hole" test. We had already been given physical exams from our old family doctor. This court hearing was the last step in the process.

As we squirmed outside in the car, Grandma was inside signing papers to give us away. We would be sent to the Ohio Soldiers' and Sailors' Orphans' Home in Xenia, Ohio, where we would each remain until we graduated from high school. Rick was nine, Jeannie was seven, and Jerry was four. I was five and ready to enter kindergarten the next month.

The light changed and I slowly drove on, deep in thought as I reflected upon my thirteen-year journey through the orphanage.

We Called It
The Home

Aunt Loualtha's first visit one month after we arrived
at the Home—Janice, Rick, Jerry, and Jeannie.

Admission Day

"Never say 'goodbye'—always say 'so long.' Goodbye means forever, and we will see you again soon." –Joseph Henry Hobbs, my Uncle Joe

It was time to go. I was looking out from an upstairs window as a big car pulled up in front of Grandma's house. Two older ladies got out and knocked on our door. Aunt Ruthie answered the door and talked with the ladies for a few moments before introducing them to us. She explained that they were here to drive us to the children's home. The ladies gave each of us a stuffed animal to cling to on our journey. Mine was a pink lamb; Jeannie's lamb was blue. I don't remember what they gave the boys.

I knew all about going to the children's home. There had been yet another family meeting with all of my aunts and uncles. I played under the big dining room table with my brothers, sister and some of my cousins during the meetings. There were a lot of legs and shoes, and we giggled as we tried to figure out whose shoes and legs belonged to whom. I could tell Aunt Ruthie's shoes because she wore them every day around the house. Aunt Lenora always wore hosiery—she called them her "stockings"—and I could tell which legs were hers. Aunt Loualtha wore the black dress-up shoes she wore every day to her job at the office. All the men had either brown or black shoes, and I couldn't tell whose shoes were whose. There must have been ten or twelve people around the table, and I overheard their whispers, "Now what are we going to do with the kids?" In my family, "the kids" always meant me and my three siblings.

My mother got sick about the time I was born. I was always told she had a nervous breakdown. I've since come to realize that she most likely had postpartum depression from which she never completely recovered. Because doctors did not yet know how to treat this condition, she was admitted into a state-run mental hospital when I was about six months old and she was already pregnant with Jerry. Other than leaving the hospital for a few weeks when Jerry was born, she remained in that same state hospital for twenty-five years. My father left us when my mother was hospitalized. I was always told he "flew the coop." It wasn't until I was older that I understood what that phrase meant. In my mind I always pictured a big white duck with his wings spread, making a noisy fuss as he flew over his baby ducklings. I never really got to know him, and saw him only a few times after we were in the Home.

We kids moved in with our maternal grandma and my mother's older sister, Loualtha, who still lived at home. Grandma took care of us while Loualtha worked and supported us financially. My older cousins spent many weekends helping Grandma give us baths and clean the house. This worked well for a few years until Loualtha married, quit working, and moved in with her new husband, Joe. By then, Grandma's health was failing—that's when the first of the family meetings was held. At that meeting it was decided that Uncle Robert, my mom's oldest brother, and his wife, Aunt Ruthie, would move into Grandma's house along with their three teenaged children. Uncle Robert worked while Ruthie took care of us four kids, her own three teenagers and her failing mother-in-law. Rick, Jeannie, and my older cousins went to school during the day while Jerry and I stayed home with Ruthie. Ruthie must have been busy taking care of her family, my family and Grandma, but she also spent precious time reading, singing, and rocking Jerry and me. I loved living with Ruthie.

"No! I'll find a way to keep them all together."

Ruthie took care of us for about a year, but raising her own family, nurturing the four of us, and nursing her ailing mother-in-law became overwhelming. Before long it was time for another family meeting. And here we were again under the table, counting shoes and giggling, oblivious to the serious discussion going on above us.

An aunt said, "We'll take the girls. They can help out around the house."

An aunt and uncle with two boys wanted to take the boys. "They can all play together, and we have plenty of boys' clothing."

"I'm not raising that bastard's kids," one uncle, referring to my dad, said. "He can raise his own damn kids."

I didn't hear that uncle's words. I'm glad I wasn't told about them until I was an adult. Soon after, this uncle-by-marriage also "flew the coop," leaving his own wife and daughter. I never saw him again. I only felt love, comfort and support from the rest of my family.

"No!" said Loualtha. "I'll find a way to keep them all together."

A few weeks later, here we were again under the dining room table for the final meeting, after which the four of us were told we would be going to a children's home. It would be a wonderful place with lots of other children to play with, all the toys we could ever want, and the four of us would still see each other all the time.

"Can we go tell the neighbors?" Rick asked. It was a rainy afternoon, but we were excited and couldn't wait to share our news.

I wonder how the adults around the table felt about the neighbors finding out where we would be going. I'm pretty sure that most of them already knew our circumstances. No one in my family ever told me how they felt at the time, but they made the children's home sound so good that we kids were truly excited about going.

"Of course, go ahead," said Loualtha.

The four of us ran to each house in our neighborhood and announced, "We are going to a children's home. We'll have a lot of other children to play with and all the toys we want."

The family across the street had eight children, and when we told our story, that mom said, "That sounds wonderful. I wish I could send my kids to a children's home!" I thought she must've been the best mother in the whole world.

Shortly before we were to leave for the Home, Grandma became quite ill and was put in the hospital. I don't know what was wrong with her, but I've often wondered if she just had a broken heart over our leaving. Loualtha took us to the hospital to visit and to say our goodbyes.

"Hi Grandma," I said slowly walking up to her bed. She looked so old and small lying in that big hospital bed.

"Hi Jeannie," Grandma held out her hand to me.

"I'm not Jeannie, I'm Janny!" I quickly corrected her. Grandma didn't have her glasses on and couldn't tell that it was me. I had no way of knowing that that would be the last time I would see Grandma.

And now these strangers were here to take us to the children's home.

"Rick and Jeannie, you two have to look out for Janice and Jerry and for each other. Remember, all you have are each other. Your brothers and sisters are the most important people in your lives," said Loualtha as she hugged us goodbye. "Joe and I will come to visit you just as soon as you are settled."

I don't remember much more about leaving and saying goodbye. I know that Loualtha and Ruthie were there, but were there others? I don't remember if I cried. I didn't want to leave, but Rick and Jeannie didn't seem to be upset, and I always tried to follow their lead.

I have often wondered how my family felt as we drove away. Were they sad? Relieved? A little of both? We must have been a handful, four children under the age of ten.

After an all-day drive, we arrived at the Home. We were met by a social worker, Miss Mildred Blair, who told us she was taking us to the Home's hospital to begin a two-week quarantine period. Miss Blair was a quiet, middle-aged woman with dark hair and glasses. She wore no makeup and was dressed rather frumpily with dark, clunky shoes.

"Why are we going to the hospital?" I asked Miss Blair. "We aren't sick."

While riding in her car to the Home's hospital, we passed at least two different playgrounds on the way. One had little girls playing outside on a merry-go-round. The other playground had a large baseball field, but there were no kids in sight.

"Why can't we stop and play with the little girls on the merry-go-round?" I wondered, disappointment washing over me. I thought we were going to play with a lot of kids and have a lot of toys, not go to a hospital.

Arriving at the Home's hospital across the street from the big baseball field, Miss Blair told us we could get out of the car.

"All new children spend their first two weeks in our hospital just to make sure they are healthy and ready to live with the other children," she explained as we walked into a pretty brick building.

A nurse wearing a white dress, white shoes, and a white hat greeted us in the lobby.

"This is the Daulbaugh Family—Rick, Jean, Janice and Jerry," announced Miss Blair as she introduced us to the nurse who was awaiting our arrival.

"Follow me," instructed the nurse, leading us down a hallway. "It's almost time for supper."

We were put in a room with four big hospital beds. Around the ceiling were paintings of Snow White and the Seven Dwarfs. I recognized the familiar characters from our story book, and liked all of them except for the witch. She was scary and mean-looking, and she terrified me; I tried to not look her direction. In my bed that night I cried and cried. I wanted Ruthie. Little did I know it would be a full year before I would see her again. I heard someone else in the room crying, too, but I never knew who it was.

I don't remember many details of the next two weeks as we were bathed, checked for head lice, given physical and dental exams, and vaccinations. Jeannie and I received awfully short ugly haircuts, parted down the middle on top with short, crooked bangs. We looked as though someone had set a soup bowl on our heads and started cutting. Rick and Jerry were given buzz cuts, and had hardly any hair left at all.

We ate our hospital meals at a little table right in our room, served by a lady from the kitchen staff. We were told that we must eat every single bite of food on our plate, even liver. Ruthie never made me eat more than a taste of liver because she knew I didn't like it. Ruthie used to laugh because I would say, "I don't like this river." At the Home they didn't laugh—they told me to eat every single bite of it. Jeannie and Rick liked liver, and when no one was looking they ate mine for me.

"Why can't we stop and play with the little girls on the merry-go-round?"

During our quarantine period in the hospital, the Home's psychologist, Miss Dorothy Hilty, took us to her tiny little office in the school building where she administered her own psychological and IQ tests. I liked Miss Hilty. She was extremely short, friendly, and didn't seem quite so intimidating to me as other adults. I was too young back then to realize that she was a dwarf. She drove us around the campus in her personal car, which was rigged so that even with her short legs she was able to reach the pedals. She pointed out where we would be living, playing and going to school. A few years later it was quite a milestone day for me when I realized I was now taller than Miss Hilty!

We met several other new kids, "newkies," also serving their two-week quarantine period. Ray was one of these newkies who seemed almost as though he was a grown-up to me. He had his own typewriter and spent a lot of his spare time typing. I loved to watch him, even though I had no idea what he was typing.

"How do you make the typewriter go so fast without looking?" I asked him. "Do you know how to play the piano?"

I couldn't play the piano, but I loved pianos and hoped to play someday.

"Yes, I can play the piano," I responded.

"Well, typing is a lot like playing the piano."

I was determined from that point on that someday I would learn to both type and play the piano.

Ray was seventeen, and in the Home only for his upcoming senior year of high school. He was placed in the senior boys' cottage, and I don't remember ever running into him again.

Two other newkies in quarantine were Emma and Ella, teenaged sisters who spent free time with us. They sneaked us outside through the hospital basement.

"That's the playground for little kids; you'll be playing there soon," said Ella as she pointed out a distant playground where lots of little children were noisily playing.

Emma and Ella also played hide and seek with us in the hospital's massive basement, and helped make our time in the hospital somewhat more pleasant. Their quarantine period ended before ours. They were placed in cottages for older girls on the main campus, so I rarely saw them. But our friendship was special, and they always had a hug and bright hello whenever we did run into each other.

I can't say I enjoyed being in the hospital, but it felt safe because the four of us were together with Rick and Jeannie looking out for us. One morning we were told we could "go down." We were released from the hospital and sent to our cottages to join the other children. My cottage was in Peter Pan, an area for the youngest children. Jerry would be in Pan 3, I in Pan 6, and Jeannie in Pan 7. Rick was placed in another area, a junior campus cottage called Taylor A.

The Home Whistle... and Bells

We didn't need a watch—we had the Whistle!

All children who passed through the Home gates have one common memory. No matter the era, the superintendent, supervisor or teacher, they had one "voice of authority." From our very first day until our very last, it awoke us in the morning, called us to meals, sent us to school, reminded us to come in from play, and sent us to bed.

The Home was kept on schedule by a loud steam whistle which blew at scheduled times throughout the day. The whistle was loud enough that residents in Xenia could hear it, and I've heard that some even planned their days around it as well.

1st Whistle at 6:20 a.m. Wake-up call. Time to jump out of bed and start the day. On Sundays we slept in, so the whistle didn't awaken us until 6:55 a.m. What a treat!

2nd Whistle at 6:40 a.m. Breakfast detail. The call to duty for girls who served breakfast as their assigned dining room detail chore.

3rd Whistle at 6:55 a.m. Call to breakfast. No matter the weather, the children who lived on main and junior campuses walked to the main dining room for each meal. The doors to the dining room did not open until 7:00 a.m. so there was no sense in arriving early, especially when it was raining, snowy or cold. Peter Pan children ate in their own little dining room, so the weather was not an issue for them.

4th Whistle at 7:50 a.m. Call to school. The Home had its own accredited K-12 school on campus. All grades were housed in a single large building; a second building housed our vocational school. We had ten minutes to get to our classrooms. No child had more than a ten-minute walk to school.

School bell at 8:00 a.m. Start of the morning session.

School Bell at 11:00 a.m. School recess for lunch.

5th Whistle at 11:15 a.m. Detail. The call to duty for girls who served lunch as their assigned dining room detail chore.

6th Whistle at 11:25 a.m. Call to lunch. This was our largest meal of the day. We did not have assigned seats, however, cottage groups sat together at assigned tables with their supervisors. Students who were "in trouble" for breaking the rules often found themselves sitting next to their supervisor. No one wanted that!

7th Whistle at 12:50 p.m. Call to school. We again had ten minutes to return to our classrooms.

School Bell at 1:00 p.m. Start of the afternoon session.

School Bell at 3:00 p.m. End of elementary day. This bell dismissed school for the elementary grades. These students would walk back to their Peter Pan cottages. One hour to go for the rest of us.

School Bell at 4:00 p.m. End of school day.

8th Whistle at 5:45 p.m. Detail. The call to duty for girls who serve supper as their assigned detail.

9th Whistle at 6:00 p.m. Call to supper. This was the signal to go to the dining room for our evening meal.

10th Whistle at 6:30 p.m. CQ (Call to Quarters). The Call to Quarters whistle changed according to the length of the day. It blew at 6:30 p.m. during the school year as our reminder to go directly to our cottages after supper, because we did not play outside in the evening on school nights. However, in the summer the CQ whistle blew as late as 9:00 p.m. when we could stay outside until dark. When the evenings were especially long due to Daylight Savings Time, we were allowed to stay out on the playground even past CQ.

11th Whistle at 9:00 p.m. Lights Out, Bedtime. This was the final whistle of the day, and signaled bedtime for the younger children on main campus. Only one whistle blew at 9:00 p.m. on the long summer evenings when CQ coincided with bedtime.

Sundays and holidays offered a different whistle schedule. We slept in a little bit longer, and whistles blew for church, a later lunch at 12:00 p.m., a 3:00 p.m. call for boys to dress in their military uniforms and assemble at the Armory, and a 4:15 p.m. call for the Sunday Military Retreat on the parade ground.

There were also special whistles for particular events. Two short blasts followed by one long blast meant fire, flood, riot or emergency. One long blast meant a child was missing or had run away. I don't remember either special whistle ever being blown.

The whistle was a constant presence in my life at the Home. It didn't care if I wanted to sleep in for ten more minutes, read just one more page, put away the Monopoly game, or fix my hair. The Whistle was always on time and our daily activities were authoritatively governed by it.

Peter Pan

"Childhood is a short season." –Helen Hayes

Peter Pan was a charming one-story, brick, horseshoe-shaped building which housed the youngest children at the Home. White wooden shutters outlined the windows with beautiful owls carved into the wood. Wrought iron accents of children at play brightened the front of the building, and a weathervane adorned the roof. The building was divided into six cottages, or Pans, with an administrative and dining area in the center. Pans 1, 2 and 3 were boys' cottages. Pan 4 was the dining room and administrative area. Pans 5, 6 and 7 were girls' cottages. A second floor above the administrative area provided housing for several employees.

The architecture in Peter Pan was fascinating. Everything in the building was scaled-down for small children. The bathrooms had tiny, low sinks with little mirrors, and tiny toilets which sat close to the floor with no doors. The showers were low on the wall, just the right height for little people. The bathtub was built higher into the wall so an adult could easily bathe a child without bending over, and had built-in steps so a child could climb in and out easily. Little tables and chairs sized perfectly for children filled the Peter Pan dining room.

Each cottage had a playroom with built-in toy boxes lining the walls, a living room with a piano and a television, and living quarters for the supervisor. All the children slept in a one-room dormitory in trundle beds lined up

Peter Pan Building showing the administrative area and Pan 5 on the right.

against the walls, each covered with a white bedspread decorated with a Sunbonnet Sue appliqué. A shared dresser sat between the beds and was used for folded clothing. No pillows were allowed while I lived in Peter Pan. We were required to sleep on our tummy with our sheet over our head to discourage any goofing around.

Peter Pan seemed dark to me. The windows seemed to let in only a tiny bit of light. The hallways were painted a dark amber as I recall, and had no windows. The locker room/bathroom had frosted windows covered on the outside by tall bushes. The dormitory had curtains drawn over the windows, as did the living room. Only the playroom saw any sunshine at all, at least in my memory.

We children were placed in cottages by age, with fifteen or sixteen children in each cottage. A locker to store hanging clothes, shoes and personal belongings was assigned to each child. These lockers were also used for time-outs when that punishment was deemed necessary.

Ms. Florence Melvin was the Dean of the Peter Pan cottages. She was a no-nonsense, heavyset older woman with gray hair pulled up into a bun on top of her head. Her office was in the administrative area, and she lived in an apartment behind her office. Placed on her desk was a ceramic loaf of bread. The center was hollowed out and filled with little Bible verse cards. Miss Melvin allowed children visiting her office to pick out a card and read the verse to her. She had her own special table in the dining room, covered with a linen tablecloth and brightened with a flower in a vase. Her big fluffy cat, Sylvia, freely roamed the halls of Pan 4.

I arrived in Pan 6 and met my supervisor, the lady in charge.

"Hello, Janice," the lady said as she looked down at me. "I'm your new mommy. You are to call me Mommy Carmen. Welcome to Pan 6."

Mommy Carmen was young, in her early 20s, and pretty with long black hair and piercing dark eyes. I didn't know my real mommy back then, so I didn't mind calling this lady "Mommy." This was extremely hard, a constant battle, for some children who had a mother they knew and loved and who, for whatever reason, was unable to care for them.

All of the girls had the same haircut that I had been given—parted down the middle with short bangs and a short bowl cut. The same barber, Mr. Vernon Nared, cut everyone's hair, even the boys', who each sported that buzz cut. I was given new black and white saddle shoes—the same shoes that all the other girls wore—as well as hand-me-down clothes for play, school, dining room and Sundays. Only dining room clothes could be worn to meals. We even changed clothes at lunchtime during the school day so that our school clothes would stay nice. All of our clothes were marked with our initials, using a black permanent marker. Jeannie and I had the same "JD" initials, and even though we were not in the same cottage, we had to use different initials for the campus laundry. We used our middle names, Elaine and Kay, so Jeannie's initials were "JED" and mine "JKD."

At mealtimes we lined up by twos to walk to the dining room. We held our partner's hand with one hand and used the other hand to place a finger over our lips to remind ourselves to not talk or make noise. Noise was discouraged in Peter Pan. I looked forward to mealtimes because I could see Jerry, and I always said hi as he walked by. His supervisor was Mommy Rhinehart, a large German woman. She always said hello to me, too. I don't remember seeing much of Jeannie in the dining room.

One day, Jerry didn't come in with his cottage group. Mommy Rhinehart leaned over and whispered "Jerry is in the hospital. He broke his arm playing Superman. He tried to fly from the top of the sliding board, and landed on his arm." The next time I saw him he was sporting a pretty blue cast. I don't think he ever tried to fly again after that!

I want to note, Jerry did not like Mommy Rhinehart, and carried ill feelings towards her throughout his life. However, she was always nice to me. Some supervisors always seemed to be nicer to folks from outside the cottage than to the children in the cottage. Jerry always told me that was true for Mommy Rhinehart; I believed him.

After lunch we walked back to our cottage and were told that it was nap time. Wait a minute—I was five years old. In my family—it was a rite of passage—when you reached five years of age you no longer had to take a nap.

"Mommy Carmen, I'm five now so I don't have to take naps anymore," I announced.

"In Peter Pan, everyone who isn't in school takes a nap. Now put on your pajamas and get into bed." Mommy Carmen clearly didn't know about the nap rule for 5 year olds.

I was heartbroken and confused. Where was Aunt Ruthie? She would make these strange people understand that I'm five. Miss Melvin, the Dean, was called and told that I wouldn't take my nap. She came to my cottage, held me in her arms in a big rocking chair and rocked me to sleep. That got me through the first day, but it didn't ever work for me again when I cried at nap time. Spankings became the order of the day until I caught on and took my naps willingly. I may have gone to bed more willingly, but I didn't sleep...ever.

Nap times meant very long afternoons for me. To this day, I still do not take naps. While we were lying down our supervisor would occasionally take a break to go into town, and Miss Maxine, the Peter Pan housekeeper, took charge of us until our supervisor returned. She sometimes caught us messing around and not sleeping. She was a strong black woman, and she spanked the offender with her bare hand. I felt the sting of her bare hand more than once, and I tried to always stay in Miss Maxine's good graces.

There were several African American girls (referred to as "colored girls" back then) in my cottage. They grew up with us, lived in the same cottages, ate meals and went to school with us. I didn't notice our differences except these girls needed their hair fixed differently from mine. Every Saturday morning Miss Maxine took these girls to a place in the basement that she had set up as a little beauty shop. She washed their hair, applied a generous amount of peach pomade, and then used some kind of hot iron to straighten their hair.

She sometimes accidentally burned someone with the hot iron, and the smell of the peach pomade combined with burnt hair and burnt skin permeated the cottage. I always felt sorry for these girls and was glad that Miss Maxine didn't need to fix my hair.

Whenever someone in the cottage had a birthday, Mommy Carmen woke us up from nap time by singing "Happy Birthday." We usually knew who was having a birthday that day and we happily shouted out her name at the proper point in the song. One day, we all sang along but no one knew whose birthday it was, and at that place in the song we fell silent. Mommy Carmen filled in the name, Clara. Clara was so surprised. She didn't know that it was her birthday until then. I knew my birthday, and felt sad that no one had told Clara when it was her birthday.

After nap time we made our beds, got dressed, were each given one piece of candy from the candy jar, and sent out to play until time to get ready for supper. All the girls from Peter Pan played on one side of the playground while the boys played on the other. I got to play with Jeannie every day during playground time. We usually played on the swings and merry-go-round. I met the older girls in Jeannie's cottage, and they let me play with them, too.

On cold, rainy, or wintry days we played in the playroom instead of going outside. We each had our own wooden toy box to store our personal toys. I remember having doll babies and books in mine. I liked to look at books and play with my dolls. We colored at the big table in the center of the room. My favorite playtime activity was playing dress-up. A cupboard that sat in a corner was filled with old lady dresses, hats, shoes and purses. I spent many hours along with the other girls dressing up in these clothes.

Behind Peter Pan was a huge concrete wading pool about a foot deep, where we swam in the summer. I couldn't play with Jerry on the playground, but we could swim together in the Peter Pan pool.

During my first year or two in Peter Pan, we enjoyed pony rides. Helen was an old Shetland pony who lived at the Home farm. She was an awfully patient animal who didn't seem to mind at all as she gave rides to any child who wanted a turn. She was old, and she died during my second or third year at the Home. Shortly before I graduated and left, four new ponies were given to the Home for the younger children to ride and enjoy.

Peter Pan children enjoying the wading pool on a hot summer day.
The Peter Pan dining room is behind the pool.

"Here, chick-chick-chicks. Here, chick-chick-chicks!" Mommy Carmen called as she stood at the back door, letting us know it was time for her Pan 6 girls to come in from the playground. I thought that was funny, kind of like a farmer calling for his chickens at feeding time.

Mommy Carmen was extremely religious, and spent at least a half hour every evening leading us in devotions. She put a lot of thought into making our devotions interesting and fun. We memorized the books of the Bible, and had Bible drill contests to see who could find a particular Bible verse the fastest. We also had contests memorizing Bible verses. Lucy usually won both of these contests. I tried, but just couldn't seem to beat her. One time Mommy Carmen awarded prizes for the winners of the Bible drill. Lucy came in first place and was given a beautiful white, lacy blouse. I was second place and received a Bible story book.

During devotions, Mommy Carmen taught us numerous Bible songs to sing. She told stories about a little boy, Jose, from the Andes Mountains in South America, by using cutout figures on a felt board. I don't remember the stories and their lessons anymore, but I loved listening and watching her as she moved the cutouts of Jose and his donkey through the mountains.

Sometimes Miss Olga Thomas, the Peter Pan dining room supervisor, joined us for devotions. Miss Thomas had also been in the Home when she was a little girl, and it was a special treat to have her spend the evening with us. She told a story about a little black sheep. She would have stopped by the cottage earlier in the day and hidden little cut-out felt sheep; one of them was black. We would search for the hidden sheep with a prize going to the girl who found the black one. We would then sing a song about a little black sheep who didn't stay with his flock, and got lost when darkness fell.

Sometimes in the evening we watched television for a little while before bedtime. Mommy Carmen required us to take turns rubbing her feet while watching television. I tried to avoid this task, and would duck down so as not to be seen. Maybe she wouldn't notice me and I could skip this dreaded assignment, but that seldom worked. The consequence for ducking out was that I usually got an extra turn.

At breakfast in Peter Pan we were always served cereal and some kind of fruit. Mommy Carmen required us to mix whatever fruit was served with the cereal of the day. This sometimes worked out well—oatmeal and raisins or Cheerios and bananas. But I'll never forget Wheaties and applesauce. What a combination, especially after adding milk! Thinking about it today makes me laugh, but back then I thought it was horrid.

Mommy Carmen insisted we have totally clean plates at the end of each meal. She taught us to squash every last pea or bean with our fork and then eat it. This became such a habit for me that I have carried it over into my adult life. Sometimes my husband or grown children remind me that I'm doing it again, and that it's not important to have my plate be so spotlessly clean. Occasionally my husband laughingly uses my plate as an example, challenging everyone else to try to get their plates as clean as mine. Old habits are hard to break!

Not all of my Peter Pan memories are good ones. One day when I was in first grade I got in trouble with Mommy Carmen. I don't remember what I did.

"Janice, when you get home from school this afternoon, you're getting a spanking," promised Mommy Carmen.

I worried about that impending spanking all day long, and I had an accident in my pants at school. When I got back to the cottage, Mommy Carmen started to spank me as promised.

After a few whacks with the paddle she scolded, "I don't think you're feeling this. Pull your pants down."

She saw the mess in my pants and really let me have it—bare. After she finished, my bottom became completely black and blue.

The next day Mommy Carmen and I were called to Miss Melvin's office, where she proceeded to turn me over her knee. I thought Miss Melvin was going to spank me, and I was already black and blue.

"Please," I begged, "don't hit me anymore!"

Miss Melvin replied, "I won't hit you. I just need to see how badly you've been hurt."

Seeing my black and blue bottom, Mommy Carmen explained, "I didn't really spank Janice that hard. Her pants were wet, and that caused the bruising to occur more easily."

Hmm. I didn't believe Mommy Carmen's explanation, but I assumed Miss Melvin did. The following day Mrs. Mart, my first grade teacher, called me out of class and told me that anytime I needed to go to the restroom to just let her know. Then she gave me the biggest hug I was given during my thirteen years in the Home. I will never forget that hug nor the love and security I felt at that moment.

One of Mommy Carmen's most common punishments was to make us sit in our locker for long periods of time with a bar of homemade laundry tar soap in our mouths. The soap barely fit in my mouth, and it caused sores on my lips and in the corners of my mouth.

I had a problem with wetting my bed, and Mommy Carmen made me wear a diaper contraption, a "damper," to bed. It had rubber pants with cotton material folded inside and ties on the sides. It was bulky and uncomfortable. The plastic covering was old and cracked, and cut into my thighs. I started taking it off in the night, praying that I wouldn't wet my bed so I could stop wearing it. Sometimes I would wake up just as I was wetting my bed. I would frantically fan my sheets in the hope that they would be dry by morning, but that never seemed to work. Somehow Mommy Carmen always seemed to know. One time Mommy Carmen made me wear the damper to school. Another time she made me wear it out on the playground with just a t-shirt as extra punishment and humiliation.

I never felt as though the other kids made fun of me when I wore the damper, but rather that they felt sorry for me. However, despite that, I learned quickly that when one of us was being punished, we were shunned by the other children who wouldn't even look at us. Perhaps they were afraid of being found guilty by association. I always felt sorry for anyone being punished, but also relieved that it wasn't me this time.

I ended up staying in Pan 6 with Mommy Carmen for about two years. The summer just before second grade I moved to Pan 7.

In Pan 7, my new supervisor was Rebecca Lawson and I was to call her Mommy Rebecca. After Mommy Carmen, she was like a breath of fresh air. She was young and beautiful with long black hair. I was thrilled to be out from under Mommy Carmen and have a Mommy like this one. She was still strict, but her most common punishment was just a quick smack with her hand. Luckily I wasn't on the receiving end of that hand too often. Mommy Rebecca led devotions each evening where she played the piano and sang like an angel. I decided that someday I would play the piano just as she did. I do play now, but not nearly

"Old habits are hard to break!"

so well as I remember Mommy Rebecca playing. I still occasionally think of her while playing my own piano.

Mommy Rebecca's family lived in Xenia and visited often. She had a mother, father, brothers and sisters. When they visited Mommy Rebecca, we felt as though they were visiting all of us. Some of the girls thought her brother was pretty cute and especially looked forward to his visits.

The year in Pan 7 with Mommy Rebecca passed quickly for me, and before I knew it I was transferred to a junior campus cottage, Taylor B. To both my surprise and dismay, I discovered that Mommy Carmen had transferred to Taylor B also, and would be my supervisor again for at least two more years. The disappointment that welled up in inside me was almost unbearable.

As I write this Peter Pan story, I want to mention all the little friends I made there, but my mind is blank in that regard. Of course I knew the other kids in Peter Pan with me, both boys and girls. But when I think about any one of them being a friend, no one person comes to mind. I could always find someone to play with. I look at pictures from those days long gone and I can name most of the kids in the pictures. But I have no memories of any specific, special friend. I remember that Lucy was always there and we liked to compete against each other in our Bible games. I remember that Clara had

Hair washing and showers in Peter Pan.

the bed beside me in Pan 6 when Miss Maxine caught us playing during nap time, and gave us each a smack on the bottom.

I believe that for me, in Peter Pan I was constantly in survival mode, always trying to please Mommy Carmen. Don't wet my bed. Eat all my food. Don't make any noise. Don't get in trouble. And above all else, don't make Mommy Carmen angry. I look back at those days with anxiety filling my whole being. I don't know if it was like that for others, but this is what I remember.

Receiving an Allowance

"Money is power, freedom, a cushion, the root of all evil, the sum of blessings."–Carl Sandburg

"Here she comes!" a small voice squealed excitedly.

Little girls quickly emerged from every corner of the playroom, watching with great anticipation as Miss Melvin, our Dean, wound her way through the cottage with her metal coin box jingling merrily, her ledger book in her hands. This joyful scene would be repeated monthly during my stay at the Home - it was allowance day. Cash was scarce for kids in the Home, but all our basic needs were met. We had plenty of mostly good food. We were provided with clean clothes, not always the most stylish, but that didn't really matter to us (at least not until we reached our teen years). We didn't really need much cash. Nonetheless, each child received a monthly allowance.

Miss Melvin sat down with each of us individually as she doled out our money and we signed her ledger book.

"But I can't write yet," I worriedly exclaimed as I was handed the ledger book to sign as proof that I had indeed received my cash.

"That's all right," answered Miss Melvin. "Just make an X on this line until you learn to write your name." I drew an X, proud that I knew how to do that.

Miss Melvin then handed me my money. The amount of our allowance was determined by age. As a 5-year-old in kindergarten, my monthly allowance was 10 cents. Although this may not seem like a lot today, it was a fortune to me, and was the only money I had ever had of my very own.

The amount each child received increased every two years. Kindergarten, 1st and 2nd graders received 10 cents; 3rd and 4th graders received 20 cents; 5th and 6th graders received 40 cents; 7th and 8th graders received 60 cents; 9th and 10th graders received 80 cents; 11th and 12th graders received a whole $1.00.

In younger cottages, the supervisors collected our dimes and set the money aside to save for a group treat—perhaps a big watermelon or ice cream for everyone. When we were old enough to move out of the Peter Pan area and onto the main campus (usually about 12 years old), our supervisor held our money for safekeeping, and doled it out to us when requested. The 40 cents by then burned a hole in my pocket, as I spent this money over and over again in my head. By the time I moved to the last two older cottages, I was able to keep my own allowance to spend as I chose.

Just outside of the Home gates stood a little convenience store aptly nicknamed by Home kids as "The Gate Store." Many, many allowances were spent there. The Gate Store sold big dill pickles from a huge wooden crock for ten cents each. I loved those big juicy pickles, and bought one whenever I could.

The junior class, as a year-round fundraising project, sold candy bars around campus. Once or twice a week, the "Candy Girl" made her rounds, and I always tried to save a dime or two for a candy bar. Many times my sister Jeannie and I would combine our money. We would buy one pickle and one candy bar to share. Nothing had ever tasted better to me.

As time passed, I discovered that receiving an allowance at the Home was not all fun and games. There was one big downside—eyeglasses. Lots of us kids wore glasses, and glasses tended to break. Mine broke one time when another girl was just being mean and stepped on them. Our broken glasses were repaired for us, but we had to pay for the repair with our allowance, which was cut in half until the bill was paid. Luckily, I didn't need to wear glasses until 7th grade when my allowance was sixty cents per month, so losing half the amount still left me with a little cash. I was never sure about the dollar amount I was required to pay back. It seemed as though I didn't receive a full allowance for a very long time. By the time my allowance had increased to $1.00, my debt had been paid and I was receiving the whole amount.

I left the Home with the conviction that I must always be able to take care of myself; that I can never rely on someone else to take care of me. For the next forty-three years I held a job, even working part-time when my children were little. Money means security to me. I'm content knowing there is enough money each month to cover living expenses, emergencies, retirement, and still have enough cash in my pocket to buy that occasional dill pickle or candy bar.

I'm still a little angry at that mean girl for stepping on my first pair of glasses! By the way, she turned out to be one of those children who just disappeared one day. I've never heard anything about her or her brother since they left.

A Self-Sufficient Operation

"Start where you are. Use what you have. Do what you can." –Arthur Ashe

The Home strived to operate as self-sufficiently as possible with its own farm, butcher shop, laundry, tailor and mending shops, shoe shop, greenhouse, water tower, heating and steam operations. Students were trained and assisted in many of these operations.

Much of our food came from the farm which was operated by employee farmers. Hogs and cows were slaughtered and sent to our butcher shop to hang and be processed. A herd of dairy cows produced our butter and milk, the freshest and best milk I've ever had. The farmers grew vegetables: beets, cabbage, carrots, corn, cucumbers, green beans, lettuce, peas, peppers, pumpkins, radishes, tomatoes, and turnips. An overhead irrigation system was used during periods of no rain to water these veggies. We often took walks to the farm's small apple orchard from Peter Pan to pick our own apples, always a tasty treat.

Both of my brothers were assigned to work at the farm at one time or another, as were most of the boys in the Home. They often talked about pitching hay and shoveling manure. I'm not sure what other chores they were assigned. Girls were not permitted to work at the farm while I was in the Home, but after I left that rule was relaxed, and girls could help out, too.

At the Home butcher shop the butcher was also a state employee. The butcher shop was located on the ground floor of the dining room, with windows facing the girls' playground, where from outside we could see the butchers at work preparing our meat. We girls thought it was disgusting to see sides of beef hanging in the shop.

We were fortunate to have a full service laundry on campus. There were about ten paid employees working here full-time. Dirty laundry for the Peter Pan children was placed in large canvas baskets on wheels. Each week, according to an established schedule, the boys on truck detail picked up these laundry baskets full of dirty clothes and delivered them to the laundry. Once there, the clothing would be washed, dried, ironed, folded, and sent back to the appropriate cottage within a day or two. This laundry service was also provided to the junior campus children, the younger children on main campus as well as the older boys on main campus. High school girls were required to do their own laundry and ironing, but we were able to send our sheets and towels to the laundry. Sports uniforms, dining room linens and hospital linens were also washed at the laundry. Employees could have their personal laundry done for them. I don't know if this was a free service or not.

One hot summer, I was assigned to help out in the laundry for a couple of days. My assignment was to help iron sheets. We used a large "ironing mangle machine" that was at least 8 feet wide. Another girl and I fed the sheets into the mangle while an employee on the other end quickly grabbed them as they came out from the other end and folded them. This was a new experience for me, one that I enjoyed, except for the heat and humidity. The laundry had to have been the hottest place on campus.

There was also a tailor shop on campus. Three women were employed here, and they mended and altered our clothing. These talented ladies also made our towels, sheets, shower curtains, pillowcases, chair covers and drapes used around the Home.

Mr. Montgomery operated the shoe shop on campus during my earlier years in the Home. He also taught shoe repairs as a vocation. He fitted us girls with our state-issued black and white shoes as well as our Sunday black flats. The shoe shop always had the most delightful smell of leather, that new shoe smell. The boys were each issued a pair of everyday brown shoes and Sunday black shoes. Mr. Montgomery re-soled and re-heeled our shoes over and over until we had outgrown them.

I'll never forget the sign that hung on the wall of his shoe shop: "I had no shoes and complained, until I met a man who had no feet."

Mr. Jandes replaced Mr. Montgomery during my senior year. The boys in his class made a variety of leather items like wallets and key chains to sell to students, employees and visitors.

Mr. Jackson, our horticulturist, grew the beautiful flowers at the greenhouse that were seen and used around campus. He provided our Memorial Day baskets that were filled with beautiful, fragrant peonies. The Chapel was adorned each week with snapdragons and chrysanthemums from the greenhouse. His poinsettias filled the dining rooms with Christmas beauty. Each meal Miss Melvin expected to see a freshly cut flower in a pretty vase on her table in the Peter Pan dining room. I'm not sure, but I'll bet her flowers were grown in our greenhouse too.

Mr. Jackson also grew vegetables such as cabbage, eggplant, peppers, sweet potatoes, and tomatoes, as well as geraniums, baby tears, a rubber plant, and orange, lemon and mango trees in the greenhouse—all available for purchase by employees and visitors.

While the State of Ohio provided just about anything we children needed, the Home was as frugal as possible and was able to obtain some products for a very low cost, or even for free. These are some of the products I remember using:

- Proctor & Gamble Unlabeled Toothpaste. (Crest, my guess provided for free.)
- Proctor & Gamble Prell Shampoo.
- Fresh Cream Deodorant. Applied with our fingertips. I can still smell that disgusting lingering scent.
- Generic Soap.
- Black Tar Soap. I always believed this soap was made somewhere at the Home, but I'm not sure.
- Toilet Paper. Cheap, rough, and felt like newsprint.
- Feminine Napkins. Modess Pads. Johnson & Johnson also provided each of us girls with a little pamphlet telling us what to expect as we entered puberty, with the reminder, "Modess. Rhymes with Oh Yes!"

Taylor B

"Life is a succession of lessons which must be lived to be understood." –Helen Keller

Taylor was the newest cottage on campus. It smelled fresh, new, and oh so good. Everything in Taylor B—the walls, ceilings, floors—seemed fresh and bright as compared to the older Peter Pan building. The boys' side was Taylor A, and the girls' side was Taylor B. Junior Campus was intended to be a bridge between the younger Peter Pan cottages and the main campus. Miss Melvin was the dean for the Taylor cottages as well as the Peter Pan cottages. Each Peter Pan cottage had a large dormitory where everyone in the cottage slept in the same room and was afforded no privacy at all. The layout for Taylor B was entirely different, having two dormitories with two rows of beds in each. Situated behind each bed was a closet/cubby area that included a dresser with drawers, a large mirror, and an area to hang clothes with storage both above on a shelf and below on the floor. A large bathroom had private stalls, a bathtub and a shower. At the front of the cottage was a large living room with huge picture windows on both the front and back walls. The basement held a playroom/study area, a full kitchen, and a large unfinished area.

Mommy Carmen was the same Mommy Carmen. She still led us in the same devotions, Bible drills, and songs as in Pan 6. We all practiced hard to memorize the verses to the Christmas story from the Bible, Luke 2:1-20. We also enjoyed learning many new Christmas carols. We took our little show on the road as we recited all 20 of these Bible verses and sang our songs for the congregation at a Xenia Baptist church. We also performed for visitors to our cottage. We even performed for Santa Claus, the Home superintendent, and the entire Christmas Committee when they visited our cottage on Christmas Eve.

Mommy Carmen loved holidays. She was creative, and our cottage always looked beautiful and festive at Christmas. She made a huge paper snowman that hung on the wall. She covered it in some sort of curly, snowy-looking material. She also threaded cotton balls and hung them at varying lengths from the ceiling. I felt as though I was walking into a winter wonderland.

After my black and blue spanking in Pan 6, Mommy Carmen was no longer permitted to spank us on our "seater," Mommy Carmen's term for our rear end. Instead she spanked us with a ping pong paddle on our hands.

Now before each spanking, Mommy Carmen took my hand, looked me in the eye and said, "Janice, this is going to hurt me more than it hurts you."

I never believed her then, and I still don't believe her to this day. In comparison, though, hand spankings didn't hurt nearly so much as seater spankings, and I was thankful for this small blessing.

When Mommy Carmen gave spankings, timing was all important in order to minimize the pain. She spanked me until I cried; however, if I cried too soon it didn't count. Those were crocodile tears and the spanking continued. If I cried too late, it just meant I got spanked longer. I learned to time my crying to the earliest possible moment that wasn't "too early," a talent that I perfected over the next two years living in Taylor B with Mommy Carmen.

Food became more of an issue for me in Taylor B. We now ate in the main campus dining room with the older kids, instead of in the Peter Pan dining room. The menus were different and were geared toward older children and adults. Mommy Carmen required that we take a regular-sized serving of everything, and we were to clean our plates. At that point in time, most of our meals seemed to repeat each week. Once a week, canned hominy was on the menu. I hated hominy—those white, starchy, round balls—just couldn't get it down. It became a weekly struggle for me. If I didn't take enough hominy to be considered a full serving, Mommy Carmen added another serving to my plate. She would punish me back at the cottage if I didn't finish by the time the meal was over. I usually had to skip dessert on hominy days because it took me the whole lunchtime just to manage to swallow that nasty stuff.

The day finally rolled around when Mommy Carmen had had enough. We both knew it was hominy day. I was sick with worry about it. Mommy Carmen was in a "determined to end this nonsense once and for all" kind of mood.

"Janice, if you don't eat all your hominy before the meal is over, I'm filling up an entire plate with it to take back to the cottage. Then you will sit and eat every bite until that plate is clean," she threatened.

I tried so hard to clean up my plate, and just as my cottage was getting up to leave the dining room, I stuffed the last bite in my mouth. That wasn't good enough for Mommy Carmen. She grabbed my dinner plate, filled it to the top with hominy and made me carry it back to the cottage. She put me and the hominy in a little room where brooms and mops were stored. I was told to stay in that room until that plate of cold, dry, hard hominy was eaten. There happened to be a toilet in that room, and I thought long and hard about flushing it all down. But no! The punishment would have been worse than eating the hominy, I was certain of that. I missed all of my playtime for three whole days before I finally cleaned my plate. But I did learn an extremely valuable lesson from this experience. Sitting in that room, it became clear to me that when I grew up, my children would never, ever have to even taste hominy. I would never have it in my home, not ever. And I never have.

Our two dormitory areas each had large picture windows across the far end of the wall. Mommy Carmen's apartment opened to the front wall of one side. There was an outside door at the front end of the other side, my side. My bed was the third bed from the door, right smack in the middle of the row. When it stormed, the lightning came in from both the big window and the window on the door. Lightning frightened me.

One night there was a bad storm and I was scared. I knocked on Mommy Carmen's door. She didn't answer, so I continued knocking until she finally woke up. She was furious!

"Mommy Carmen, I'm scared," I whimpered.

The lightning was flashing around us, followed immediately by loud claps of thunder.

"Don't you ever wake me up again just because you're afraid!" Mommy Carmen warned.

She sent me back to bed, a little more frightened than before. But she told me a Bible verse to recite over and over again until I wasn't afraid anymore.

She told me, "when you're afraid, just keep reciting this verse: 'What time I am afraid, I will trust in thee.' Psalms 56:3."

I'm not sure the Bible verse made me less afraid, but reciting it did help me finally fall back asleep. And I decided right then and there that when I grew up and became a mommy, my children could wake me up anytime for any reason and I wouldn't scold them. I would hold and comfort my children until they weren't afraid anymore.

Many nights, when we had all behaved, Mommy Carmen played records on her record player for us as we drifted off to sleep. Her favorite record album seemed to be theme songs from classic movies. A pleasant memory was falling asleep to the first song on the album, the theme song from "Exodus." I don't remember ever staying awake long enough to hear the following songs.

Mr. and Mrs. Owen Hacker were frequent visitors to Taylor B. Mr. Hacker had grown up in the Home many years before us. They had grown children and grandchildren of their own, yet they took us Taylor B girls under their wing, acting as pseudo grandparents. The Hackers visited often and always brought treats with them—candy, cookies, cupcakes, ice cream or popsicles. Other times they arrived with a group of friends to share a potluck dinner, and entertain us girls with songs and stories.

One Easter, Mrs. Hacker brought new matching Easter outfits for each girl in the cottage. We received a new white blouse adorned with a beautiful hand-embroidered flower, and a light blue skirt decorated with a large, uniquely designed pocket. Mrs. Hacker embroidered the blouses and handmade the

Taylor B Dormitory. My bed and closet were the third from the right with my doll lying on top.

skirts for us. Governor Michael DiSalle visited the Home while I was in Taylor B. We were thrilled to have the Governor of Ohio stop by our cottage and say hello. We each wrote him a letter of thanks for his visit, and he responded to each of us saying he hoped to return sometime. I still have my letter.

I don't remember Mommy Carmen ever using the kitchen in Taylor B. However, Mommy Klopher, the supervisor from next door in Taylor A, often made a large pan of pulled pork for after-school sandwiches for her boys. She kindly shared this treat with us girls next door, and we loved it.

Taylor B girls attended a Baptist church in Xenia. We were picked up in a bus owned by the church and driven by Brother Tucker. We went to both Sunday School and then to the adult church upstairs with Mommy Carmen. We spent many Sunday afternoons in Taylor B doing the Sunday School homework doled out by our teacher.

Mommy Carmen expected each of us to accept the minister's invitation to receive Christ as our savior, to walk up to the front of the church, give our testimony, and be welcomed by the minister and congregation. Mommy

Carmen stressed that this must come from our heart, not just to show off or to please her. I remember that in those days my whole purpose in life was to please Mommy Carmen and to avoid her wrath. And that was what was going through my mind as I walked up to the front of the congregation.

This church was taking donations for a new church building. Mommy Carmen convinced us young girls that we wanted to donate to this church's building fund. The church was selling cement blocks for the foundation of the new building at twenty-five cents per block. Mommy Carmen saved our monthly allowances, and each quarter accumulated was donated to the Church's building fund. We each bought at least three or four blocks. I was proud to make Mommy Carmen happy as she handed over our money to her church.

Election Day, November 1960. We girls were in the playroom/study area in the basement of Taylor B. Mommy Carmen came down the stairs, clutching at the wall as she descended so as to steady herself and not fall. When she reached the bottom of the stairs, she grabbed her stomach and forehead as a person fainting might do.

"The world has come to an end!" she exclaimed.

"Why, Mommy? What happened?" we all asked at once.

She responded, "A Roman Catholic has just been elected President of the United States!"

We girls were frightened. What did this mean? What would happen to us? For whatever reason, Mommy Carmen despised the Catholic religion, and in her mind this was truly a tragedy. She not only hated the religion, but she taught us little girls in her cottage to hate it, too. She taught us that Catholics worshiped the Pope instead of God, that they worshiped idols, and that they were to be both feared and hated. When Kennedy was elected President, Mommy Carmen was devastated.

Shortly after this event, I was a patient in our little Home hospital. My favorite nurse, Mrs. Morrow, was working on the afternoon shift. That particular day I noticed she was wearing a little cross pin.

"Why are you wearing that pin?" I asked. "What's it for?"

Mrs. Morrow was nice and patient. She always took a moment or two to kindly chat with me when she had time. "This is my Catholic pin," she gently explained.

"I hate Catholics!" I gasped.

She asked me why, and I told her everything I had been taught about the Catholic religion. The next day Mrs. Morrow brought in her big Catholic Bible. She sat down beside me on my bed and graciously explained about her Bible and her faith. I was extremely confused. I loved Mrs. Morrow and always would, but how could I reconcile the fact that she was Catholic?

Shortly after this, my cottage group was on the bus on our way downtown to Sunday School. Mommy Carmen was not with us this time. Miss Melvin boarded the bus and sat with my cottage group. She questioned us regarding Catholicism and what we knew about this religion. We all started talking at once, and we told her just how much we hated Catholics. Miss Melvin told us that Mommy Carmen was wrong to teach us these beliefs.

"Why are you wearing that pin?"

I came home from school one spring day, and she was gone, just like that. Mommy Carmen had left, and I didn't know why. There were no goodbyes, nothing. I had a new Mommy, Miss Irene, who said we didn't have to call her Mommy. She was young and kind. After living with Miss Irene for just a few weeks, I moved to the main campus where the older girls lived. I was genuinely relieved to leave Peter Pan and Taylor behind me.

I know Mommy Carmen was wrong, but it was hard for me to overcome the religious beliefs she had instilled in me. You can imagine my conflicting emotions when I discovered my very first boss was not only Catholic, but attended mass every single morning before work. And then my second boss, too. And some of my best friends were Catholics. And my brother-in-law. And now even my husband. So many good people in my life are Catholics. I know I will never join the Catholic Church but I have learned to appreciate and respect this religion.

My Siblings and Family

"The only people who truly know your story
are the ones who help you write it." –Unknown

When we entered the Home, we were a fairly typical family as compared to many others with younger children. There were four of us in elementary school; 4th grade, 2nd grade and kindergarten. Jerry was only 4 years old so technically not yet old enough for school. Children were typically not permitted to enter the Home before being 5 years old and kindergarten-ready, although exceptions were made in order to keep larger families together. This exception was made for Jerry, who attended kindergarten for two years so that he could join his proper class. He really hated it when I teased him about flunking kindergarten.

Because Rick was older and not assigned to live in the Peter Pan cottages, he played on an older boys' playground, ate meals in the main campus dining room, and I rarely saw him. He was four years ahead of me in school, so our paths never crossed there. I grew up feeling as though I didn't really know him.

One day Rick had an idea: "Mr. Hartpence, I've saved up a few dollars; would I be allowed to have a little picnic for my brother and sisters? I've got enough money to buy some bread, bologna and potato chips."

Mr. Hartpence was the superintendent at the time. Jerry and I were still in Peter Pan and Jeannie had moved to junior campus.

"No," Mr. Hartpence replied. "I could never allow something like that to get started."

Rick later told me that he was devastated that he couldn't give us that little picnic. I'm happy to report that after I left the Home and a new superintendent came on board, more effort was made to help families spend time together.

When I was eleven, I moved to main campus and was able to see Jeannie more often. For the first year or two we lived in the same cottage and were even roommates for a short while. When Jeannie was old enough, she took me shopping and to movies with her, a short walk into town. I loved hanging out with my big sister.

Jerry and I were in Peter Pan many of the same years. We sat together at the same kindergarten table, and both got scolded for talking too much. As we grew older, we often saw each other at school and visited together as much as we could. Once we were both in high school we took journalism class together for three years. We wrote articles together for the Home's monthly newsletter, *The Home Review*. We were able to walk all over campus together as we pursued our stories. We also saw each other at sporting events and other weekend activities.

My Aunt Loualtha and Uncle Joe took us to their home for two weeks in the summer and a week at Christmas. It was during these visits that I got to know Rick a little better. Life seemed almost normal during our family vacations as we played together, ate together, and even had sibling squabbles together.

Loualtha and Joe introduced us to their friends, Bill and Shirley Moland, who lived in nearby Dayton, Ohio. Shirley's mother and father had both been raised in the Home along with all of her aunts and uncles. Shirley's entire family had great love for the Home and met together every year during the annual Reunion for ex-pupils.

Shirley and Bill became like family to us as they took us to their home many times to visit and to play with their little girls, Karen and Cheryl. Several times they invited us to dinners and swimming at their country club. Jeannie and I attended Karen's ice skating program which featured Olympic champion Peggy Fleming. We helped Karen get Peggy's autograph, a thrill for all of us.

Seniors were permitted to take days away from school to look for jobs and housing. Although I didn't plan to be living in the Dayton area, I was still able to take these days off. I called Shirley each time, hoping to spend the day with her. She never let me down, but instead drove to the Home, picked me up, and we spent those days together having lunch and shopping.

As Rick, and then Jeannie graduated and left the Home, I was heartbroken at being left behind. I still had two more years until I graduated and could leave, while Jerry still had three years to go. As we approached our junior and senior years, Jerry and I had more opportunities to spend time together. We were able to obtain a Town Pass and walk to Xenia together to shop or go to the movies.

Aunt Loualtha's visit on our first Christmas at the Home.

After Jeannie graduated we stayed in touch through collect phone calls. A new pay phone had been installed on the girls' side near the Main Building, and I called Jeannie and Loualtha quite often. They always accepted my calls and seemed happy to talk with me.

I also spent as much time with Jeannie as I could on our family vacations with Loualtha and Joe. Jeannie started working right after graduation and had some spending money when we visited. The summer between my junior and senior years, she took Jerry and me to the Brown Derby Restaurant where she ordered us each a steak, baked potato with sour cream, and salad with Italian dressing. She explained that this is what her friends from outside of the Home liked to eat. I felt mature and refined, hopeful that someday I would have enough money to enjoy the luxury of a Brown Derby steak whenever I wanted.

Shortly before my graduation, Jerry and I received permission to go shopping in Xenia. I had some money I had earned, and wanted to do something special with Jerry before I left. We dressed up, walked to the bus station in Xenia and caught a bus to Dayton. We were not allowed to leave the downtown Xenia area, and Dayton was about 15 miles away. We would be in big trouble if we were caught. When we exited the bus, whom did we run into but a Home

Jeannie and me singing Christmas Carols in Pan 6 living room.

employee's daughter. We were caught. I knew this young girl pretty well, and asked her to please not tell on us. She said she wouldn't, and she never did.

Jerry and I looked for the nicest steak restaurant we could find within walking distance of the bus stop. We found what seemed to us to be an elegant steak restaurant; not a Brown Derby, but it would do. We were seated, and ordered steak dinners. I could feel the waiter looking at us strangely, and just after we placed our order the manager stopped by our table to demand payment before we could be served. We must have looked so very young. I paid immediately, and we had a wonderful dinner. I promised Jerry we would again have a steak dinner together on his graduation day the following year.

I was sad to leave Jerry at the Home by himself. He was a senior with only one year left until he could leave, too. With lots of letters back and forth, many collect phone calls, visits as often as possible, and a new girlfriend, he told me the year passed fairly quickly for him. And when he graduated we did have that celebratory steak dinner.

Veterans' Organizations

*"Anyone who does anything to help a child in his life
is a hero to me." –Fred Rogers*

One of the happiest, brightest days each year for all of the Home kids was 40 et 8 Day. The 40 et 8 is an elite group of veterans formed out of the American Legion. Their symbol is the French boxcar that carried ground troops to the front lines during World War I. Seven or eight 40 et 8 posts from around the state still owned these boxcars that could hold 40 men and 8 horses. These posts drove their boxcars from all over Ohio to the Home twice each year for the enjoyment of us kids.

These kind gentlemen spent the day giving us children rides around the campus in their boxcars. Over and over we would ride, the wind blowing in our hair, the sun shining in our eyes, pure joy on our faces. And candy. Plenty of candy to enjoy, both for the riders as well as anyone we passed along the way.

Later that evening, the 40 et 8 sponsored a Bingo game for grades eight and below. For high school students, these veterans sponsored a dance with live music. And, there was always cider and donuts for everyone to enjoy throughout the evening.

My life at the Home was greatly enriched by various veterans' organizations. Each cottage had a dedicated "sponsor," a veterans' organization, referred to as their "Post." Posts provided many of the extras that make life enjoyable. While not each cottage received the same goodies, these extras might include:

- Spending money, televisions, radios, record players, clocks, toasters, encyclopedias, etc.
- Picnics, birthday presents, parties, dinners, movies, trips to theme parks.
- Halloween parties, Christmas parties with presents, Valentine treats.
- Trips to Cincinnati Reds games, the Cincinnati Zoo, Coney Island, Columbus for dinner and a movie.
- Cookies, popcorn, candy, fruit, nuts.

- Clothing, socks, hosiery, coats, gloves, pajamas, slippers, formal gowns.
- Sleds, basketballs, footballs, fish-filled aquariums, pool tables, ping-pong tables, teddy bears, board games, decks of cards, puzzles, books, and magazines.
- Wastebaskets for our bedrooms, hairdryers, bathroom and bedroom throw rugs, pictures for walls.
- Perfume, powder, make-up, jewelry boxes, shaving lotion.

Some of these veterans' organizations did not sponsor an individual cottage, but provided funding for the entire Home where needed. These funds purchased:

- Christmas presents for us children. Some of the veterans' groups also helped to wrap and deliver the presents on Christmas Eve.
- Scholarships at graduation
- Money and candy for Easter baskets
- Band instruments and uniforms
- New library books
- New curtains for the main dining room
- New cheerleading uniforms
- Money for the Recreation Fund
- Money for the Entertainment Fund (used for special outings like the circus or sporting events)
- Magic shows for younger children
- Movie equipment, projectors, speaker/sound system, screen and stage curtains for the Auditorium
- New organ and carpeting for the Chapel
- New jukebox with records, new lighting, and new tables and chairs for the Orfenz Den.
- Roller skates for skating parties in the Armory
- Renovations to the Hobby Center
- Games and radios for the Hospital
- Furniture and paint for the Hospital
- Polaroid camera for the Print Shop

Members of the 40 et 8 giving boxcar rides to the Home children.

An ex-pupil, Mr. "Hat" Noland, a 1928 graduate from the Home, was the president of the Noland Paper Company in California. During my high school years, he donated a boxcar filled with 80,000 pounds of paper to the Home. This was to be used for school work, forms printed at the print shop, and programs for plays, concerts and graduations. It was used the most for the printing of *The Home Review*. They were still using this paper long after I had graduated.

Not all posts provided the same benefits. One of my favorite posts was from St. Marys, Ohio. The Auglaize County Sheriff was a member of this particular post. One sunny summer day, he provided several cruisers as well as another member's personal car, a beautiful red convertible, to drive everyone in the cottage to Grand Lake near St. Marys for a picnic. Several post members owned motor boats and spent the afternoon giving us rides around the lake. I'll never forget the fun I had that day.

Another time, this same post held a clothing drive. The members of the post surprised my teenage cottage with tons of clothing for us girls to sort through. We each ended up with at least several new outfits.

A non-veterans' group which also provided much-appreciated support was the Association of Ex-Pupils, an organization comprised of former Home students. This group supported the students with scholarships, Christmas shopping money, wrapping and delivering Christmas presents, as well as friendship and numerous other offerings throughout the year.

Many outside groups visited the Home frequently. I loved being chosen to give a tour and talk about our Home. Rev. Howard often traveled around the state visiting veterans' organizations to solicit funding for the Home. During my senior year, he often invited me and at least one other girl to travel with him to these posts to tout our Home and answer any questions presented to us.

Here are some of the veterans' organizations that made my life at the Home more enjoyable. I'm sure I've missed a group or two. I owe each one a huge thank you. I hope they knew just how much their thoughtfulness, attention and gifts were appreciated.

40 et 8
American Legion and Auxiliary
AMVETS and Auxiliary
Blue Star Mothers of America
Daughters of the American Revolution
Daughters of Union Veterans
Disabled American Veterans and Auxiliary
Ladies of the Grand Army of the Republic
Navy Club Auxiliary
Officers' Wives Club at Wright Patterson Air Force Base
Ohio Gold Star Mothers
Ohio State Grandmothers Chapters
Sons of Union Veterans and Auxiliary
United Spanish War Veterans and Auxiliary
Veterans of Foreign Wars and Auxiliary
Women's Relief Corps

Food and Dining

We offer thanks to thee, oh Lord,
For this our daily food
May we in thought and deed and word
Show forth our gratitude. Amen —Author Unknown

We offer thanks to thee, oh Lord...our prayer, recited before each meal in the Children's Dining Room at the Home. Students from the Home's Church Council took turns leading the prayer by playing a little melody on a set of chimes. I led the prayers often during my last two years at the Home. We still recite our prayer during our Association of Ex-Pupils Reunion each July.

During my stay at the Home, at least two different dietitians were responsible for menu planning. I thought that one of them made sure we were served a balanced diet, but not much thought went into planning meals that children would actually like to eat. I didn't enjoy everything that was served, but there was always plenty of good quality food.

There were four dining areas around the Home. As mentioned, the hospital and Peter Pan each had their own kitchen and dining room, while children living on the main campus ate in the main dining room. A cafeteria-style staff dining room was located in the main building annex to serve meals to administrative employees who did not eat with the children. During my later years in the Home, this dining room was also used for special occasions such as monthly birthday dinners for the children.

No matter the dining room, we children sat in cottage groups at several tables near our supervisor, who also sat at one of the tables. Tables were assigned by cottages with boys on one side of the room and girls on the other. Food was served family style with filled dishes placed on the table by girls serving dining room detail. Second helpings were almost always available, and were always offered to the boys before the girls. I'm not sure why boys got to go first, but there was usually enough left for the girls to get seconds, too. Whatever happened to the concept of "ladies first?"

I believe the Peter Pan kitchen served the best food. I didn't appreciate it at all as a little Peter Pan resident, but as a teenager working detail there I realized just how good this food was. When working on detail in the Peter Pan dining room, I spent many Saturday mornings doing extra cleaning in the dining room and kitchen as the cooks were fixing lunch, the main meal of the day. When our chores were completed, the cooks would share whatever they had prepared with us detail girls. I remember eating delicious fried chicken and pork chops, but my favorite was their homemade vegetable soup. It was the best I've ever tasted. As an adult I've tried to make vegetable soup just like what the cooks made in the Peter Pan kitchen, but mine never seems to taste quite so good as I remember. Their soup was loaded with beef, potatoes, carrots, beans, and tomatoes, and was so flavorful.

After the long-time dietitian, Mrs. Davis, retired, I don't remember ever being served hominy again. Oh happy day! The menus prepared by Mr. Gaither, our new dietitian, definitely were more kid/teen friendly.

I'll never forget the first time I ate pizza. The dining staff called it pizza pie. Today, it is still the best pizza I've ever eaten. If my memory is correct, the homemade yeast dough was smothered with tomato sauce, oregano, hamburger and cheddar cheese, then topped with a generous amount of Parmesan cheese. We each were served a huge piece that covered our plate and we could even have seconds. It was a memorable treat.

Homemade Sunday dinner rolls were everyone's favorite. They were made by Chef Ralph Wall, and later by Ms. Lillian. "The secret ingredient to the dinner rolls was Ralph Wall's sweat," Rick said. Whatever, they were delicious.

Some of my other favorites were Sunday roast beef, mashed potatoes and gravy, toast with melted painted-on butter, chili, homemade lunch soups and desserts. Once a week we had vegetable soup that included leftovers from every vegetable that was served during the previous week. Sometimes this soup was delicious. Once in a while there weren't many vegetables at all, and other times the vegetables in the soup seemed not to belong there, like canned spinach.

We were served cold cut sandwiches each Sunday evening. Rotating weeks, either potato salad or Kuntz potato chips were served as an accompaniment to the sandwiches. I was always a little disappointed on potato salad week. Kuntz potato chips were made in Xenia, and I loved them. Sadly, the Kuntz potato chip factory is long gone, and people today will never know that this is how a potato chip is supposed to taste!

We girls served detail duty in the dining room throughout our high school years. We were assigned to a 3-month schedule, with most girls serving two meals per day. We were assigned to small groups of about five girls, with an older girl designated as captain to supervise that group. Our assignments could be in the main dining room, the hospital dining room, or in the Peter Pan dining room. Detail duty could include setting tables, putting food and drinks on the tables, setting up the juice and coffee stations, or making toast. Making toast was the most fun and my favorite assignment. We continuously placed bread on a large conveyer belt toaster. The bread was carried along through the heating process, and when the toast was ready it fell out. We grabbed it and painted on melted butter with a large paint brush. It was delicious! The same girls also cleaned up the tables after the meal and swept the floors. Boys were assigned to gather, scrape and wash the dirty dishes using the large capacity, manual dishwashers. As dishes were cleaned, they were put in carts and taken out to the dining room where the detail girls put them away. The clean silverware came out of the kitchen in one big cart. It was always steaming hot. We detail girls sorted it and put it away in drawers. I got pretty good at grabbing a handful of mixed silverware and sorting it into the proper drawers, as though dealing a deck of hot cards.

About twenty minutes into the meal, a dining room supervisor signaled to detail girls that it was time for dessert. The desserts were set out in the front of the dining room. Detail girls walked up front, grabbed a tray, loaded it with desserts, and served it to each student at their assigned tables. Because I was self-conscious, I hated this task, especially if I was assigned to boys' tables. It felt as though all eyes were on us girls as we took that long walk to the front of the dining room. Looking back, I'll bet that those eyes were just trying to get a glimpse of the dessert that was being served that meal.

We got to enjoy dessert with both lunch and supper. We had ice cream for dessert at lunch on Sundays. Other desserts could be cookies, cake, pie, date nut roll, fresh fruit, canned fruit, or pudding. Watermelon was a favorite in the summertime. During my junior year, the Borden Company donated over 300 gallons of fudge ripple ice cream, enough to last for several days. What a treat!

Hospital Memories

*"Nurses might not be angels, but it's sometimes hard
to know the difference." –Anonymous*

The Home hospital was a beehive of activity with both adults and children coming and going much of the time. The hospital staff saw us Home children through illnesses, injuries, and preventative treatments, as well as physical, dental and vision checkups. A registered nurse was on duty 24-hours a day to manage this approximately 100-bed facility that also housed a clinical area, dental office, operating room, full kitchen, and staff dining room. There were two main wards with about 20 beds in each, one for girls and one for boys. At the other end of the building were two more identical wards that were seldom used. There were several shower rooms and smaller patient rooms scattered throughout the building. During our two-week quarantine period, my family stayed in one of these smaller rooms.

Three "clinics" were held at the hospital each day where sick or injured children could be seen by a nurse after receiving written permission from their supervisor. Any medications used by students were administered at the hospital, even simple things like aspirin, nose drops or band aids. The main daily clinic was held after school at 4:00 p.m. Children could ask permission to go to this clinic, and were seen for anything from splinters to athlete's foot to acne. The clinic held right after breakfast was visited mostly by children who were obviously sick and were sent by their supervisor for evaluation, although some children were there for follow-up visits or medications. The lunchtime clinic was mostly for follow-up and medications. Children who became sick during off hours were allowed to drop in at the hospital for treatment, but only after receiving written permission from a supervisor or teacher. Children with chronic or more serious illnesses were treated at larger hospitals in Xenia, Dayton or Cincinnati.

Preventative treatments provided to Home children included yearly physicals, eye exams and vaccinations. We received all the usual vaccinations from that era: Smallpox, Diphtheria/Tetanus/Pertussis (DPT) and Polio. In my younger years the polio vaccine was given by inoculation. Eventually that was changed to medicine dropped into a sugar cube. Eating a sugar cube was so much better than getting a shot!

Not surprisingly, I never wanted to be admitted to the hospital. During clinic we sick children were seated in metal chairs around the clinic room as the nurse took our temperatures. Oh, how I used to pray that my temperature would be normal. Anyone with even the slightest fever was admitted to the hospital. I hated that walk to the pajama room, a room lined with metal shelves that were filled with some of the ugliest cotton pajamas I have ever seen. No matter the nurse on duty, she would dig through all those pajamas until she found that perfect pair she seemed to be looking for.

"Here, Janice, this pair will do," the nurse would say as she handed me what appeared to me to be the most hideous pair of all. The pajamas were cotton prints made from fabric similar to today's hospital gowns, but sewn into pajamas. I believe both boys and girls wore this same style.

I was also given slippers and a brown paper bag before we made the long walk down the hall to the girls' ward. I wanted to turn and run out of the building, go any place except for the hospital.

The nurse assigned me to a bed, then said, "Go put on your pajamas, put all your clothes in this paper bag, and get in bed."

I hated those words. It was so boring in the hospital, especially if I didn't feel very sick. We were required to stay in bed except during meals, showers and for the potty. There was no television. Only teenagers could check out a radio during a few specific hours. If you were stuck in the hospital with only younger children, no radio was permitted. Each ward had a cupboard filled with books, magazines, and children's puzzles. It seemed that they were never changed, and I'm sure over the years I read every single book and magazine more than once.

Until I was older and living on main campus, we had no access to radios except when we were in the hospital. I loved listening to all the hit songs when an older girl was available to check out a radio. Most of the teenagers in the Home listened only to WING in Dayton. This was how I learned many of the hit songs that are "oldies" today. I still love to listen to them.

During one of my hospital stays, the hit song *Chances Are* by Johnny Mathis came on the radio. The teenage girl with the radio looked at me and said, "Ya know, kid, you don't have a chance at all in this world."

I wasn't exactly sure what she meant at the time, but her words stayed with me. This was a hit song in the 1957-58 time frame, so I must have been about seven years old. I wish I could tell her that she was wrong, that my life would be full of chances and choices, and today I'm happy and content.

Meals were served to patients in sunroom-type areas at the ends of each of the wards. The girls' ward was located just across the street from the older boys' cottages. Once I started feeling better, it was hard to look out the windows and see the boys going to school and meals, and living their lives while I was cooped up in the hospital in hideous pajamas. As an older patient, I could see my male friends and classmates, and that made staying in the hospital even harder for me.

The hospital had its own kitchen and cooks, and most of the meals were good. Anyone with an upset stomach was served tea, toast, and applesauce without fail. It never tasted good to me, but then nothing ever tasted good when I had an upset stomach.

The staff secretary, Ms. Weaver, also administered eye exams and fitted children for glasses. The hospital custodian, Mr. Jackson, was truly a jack-of-all trades who helped out wherever and whenever needed. Besides his custodial duties, some of his other assignments were orderly and chauffeur.

I wish I could tell her that she was wrong, that my life would be full of chances and choices....

Most of the nurses were very nice. Mrs. Neville, who was the nursing supervisor, was a strict, no-nonsense type. She was on duty Monday through Friday during daytime hours. She ran most of the daily clinics and reported to the physician who made rounds each weekday.

Ms. Moorehead was the night nurse. We rarely saw her except when someone coughed in the night. She would then walk among our beds trying to figure out who was coughing so she could give that child a teaspoon of her nasty yellow cough syrup. I tried hard to never get caught coughing, but I usually failed. Ms. Moorehead was also the nurse who awakened us, even before the 6:20 a.m. whistle, by flipping on the bare ceiling lights and instructing us to get up and wash our faces before breakfast. And then she was gone for the day.

My favorite nurse, Mrs. Morrow, remains one of the kindest ladies I've ever known. She usually worked the 3:00–11:00 p.m. shift, and often sat and visited with me. I always cherished the time she spent with me.

Mrs. Prindle was also a very kind nurse who eventually replaced Mrs. Neville, upon her retirement, as nursing supervisor. But when I occasionally went to the clinic with monthly cramps hoping for something for pain relief, Mrs. Prindle was less than sympathetic, not nearly so understanding as the other nurses. She did give me something for the pain and allowed me to lie down for an hour or so, but she also told me to just accept the cramps as part of growing up, and move on with my day. Mrs. Prindle worked mostly during the daytime hours.

There was also Ms. Fry, the oldest of the nurses. She was a little grumpy sometimes, but mostly kind. I particularly didn't like getting shots from her because her hands shook badly, and her shots seemed to hurt more than shots from the other nurses. Ms. Fry also usually worked during the daytime hours.

Mrs. Burkholder usually worked the 3:00–11:00 p.m. shift, and was my least favorite nurse. She had a little temper and it wasn't a good idea to be caught out of bed or messing around when she was on duty. She was also rougher than the other nurses when giving treatments or shots. Enemas seemed to be her favorite cure for just about any affliction, especially tummy aches. But one evening when I was a young patient, an older boy came to the hospital in great pain and was eventually diagnosed with appendicitis. I eavesdropped as Mrs. Burkholder displayed a kindness and tenderness toward him that I had never witnessed from her before. I never forgot her capacity for kindness that day.

Dr. Ellis was the physician who visited the hospital each weekday. Most of my hospital stays seemed to be for sore throats. When making his rounds, Dr. Ellis would stop by my bed, ask the nurses whether I had a temperature, and would then look at my throat. If normal, he would give the OK for me to go back to my cottage and school. But more often than not, it seemed he would shake his head and say I needed to stay in the hospital a while longer. I can still feel the sadness and disappointment—I hated being in the hospital, but Dr. Ellis's decision was final and not negotiable. Other times, adding insult to injury, he would whisper to the nurse beside him, "Sulfa" or "Penicillin."

In those days, that meant I would be receiving shots. Oh, how I hated shots with those huge needles!

When I was younger, there was a measles outbreak on campus. The hospital was packed with children. All four wings of the hospital were full, and mattresses were placed on the floors lining the hallways. As fate would have it, I ended up in the hospital, too, but with a sore throat. Once I was well, Dr. Ellis stopped by my bed every day to check my tummy for measles since I had surely been exposed. If I had them, he didn't want to release me until I was over them. But fortunately I never caught the measles. However, I still had to stay in the hospital for several weeks so as not to expose the other children back in the cottage. At that point I stopped liking Dr. Ellis, and thought he was just being mean, checking my tummy and making me stay in the hospital.

Many children had their tonsils taken out in the Home hospital. Dr. Ellis performed these surgeries with Mrs. Neville and Ms. Weaver, the staff secretary, assisting. Dr. Schuller, the dentist, served as anesthesiologist, and Mr. Jackson, the custodian, served as the operating room orderly. Luckily, I think all the children made it through these tonsillectomies just fine.

After Dr. Ellis retired, Dr. Warner took his place. I'll always remember that he wore bright red socks every single day. I was a senior with yet another sore throat when he made the decision to schedule me for a tonsillectomy. Luckily, by that time these were no longer performed at the Home hospital, but rather at Greene Memorial Hospital in Xenia, where I was taken.

The Home had a full-time dentist on staff. All of the students were given annual dental exams and cleanings as a minimum treatment. The dentist also provided fillings, and fitted children with braces as needed. The dentist in my early years was Dr. Schuller, followed by Dr. Horne. Dr. Schuller was gentle and friendly, and always greeted me with, "Hi, Snow White. How are the seven dwarfs?"

When I had my tonsils removed, I was surprised that Dr. Schuller was my anesthesiologist. And once again he used that same old line, "Hi, Snow White. How are the seven dwarfs?" just before he put me to sleep.

When I was in high school, all of the Home children were required to be part of a Proctor & Gamble dental research control group. Several times a year, dental research assistants came to the Home and provided dental exams

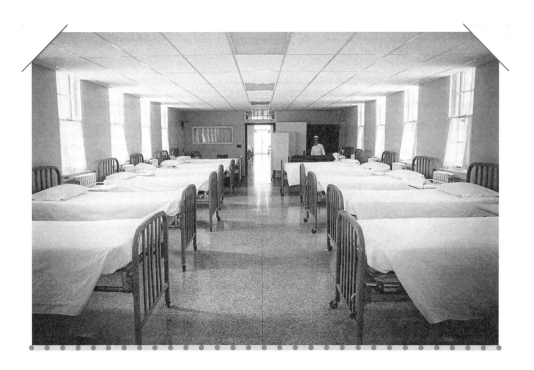

Mrs. Prindle, RN, looking after a patient at the Home hospital.

and x-rays to us children. We were an ideal control group as we were well supervised, lived the same lifestyles, and ate the same food. We each were given plain white tubes of toothpaste with either a red or blue band at the top. The toothpaste, provided free to us from Proctor & Gamble, was actually given to our supervisors to put on our toothbrushes. They were then required to observe as we brushed our teeth twice a day, no more and no less. This continued for the rest of the time I was in the Home until I was a senior. As seniors we were finally permitted to have our own tube of toothpaste and allowed to put the paste on the brush ourselves. And, some days I even brushed three times. Shhh!

I never found out the results of that research project. The study was done by the Proctor & Gamble Company in Cincinnati. We were never told the name of the toothpaste, but the only toothpaste that tastes right to me today is Crest, so I'm betting it was Crest toothpaste. I assume that Proctor & Gamble was conducting the study to research fluoride, a new concept at the time. We were never told which group, red or blue, received the fluoride.

Life on Main Campus

"Sunshine, Lollipops, and Rainbows." —Marvin Hamlisch

As I skipped along the sidewalk, the sun was shining brightly, the air was breezy and warm, the birds were chirping merrily, even the bunnies and squirrels seemed to be happy.

The day had finally arrived! I was leaving Peter Pan and Taylor B behind and moving to the main campus. I would be living in Jackson A, Jeannie's cottage. No moving vans, but instead we had boys on truck detail. I packed up my belongings in a provided cardboard box and walked to my new cottage. By the time I got there, my belongings had already been delivered.

The cottages on campus were completely different from the Peter Pan and Taylor cottages. These two-story buildings did not have dormitories, but rather real bedrooms with two girls assigned to a room. Each cottage had a large living room, basement, restrooms on each floor, and a residence area for the supervisor. There were five of these buildings on the girls' campus and five on the boys' campus. Each building, named after a president, was divided into two cottages, an "A" side and a "B" side. A locked door separated the two sides. Some of the cottages housed younger girls aged 10–15; some housed older girls aged 16–17; and there were separate cottages for senior girls and boys.

Jeannie was my first roommate, and she "showed me the ropes." She explained the rules, some of which were exclusive to Home children, while others were pretty standard for any child growing up in this era, even in a real home with real parents. It became clear to me that it was important to behave and follow rules everywhere on campus. You see, the employees talked. If you were in trouble in one area of campus, you were in trouble everywhere. Here are some of the new rules I quickly learned.

- A formal room inspection was conducted every Wednesday while we were at school. The inspection team was comprised of the Dean of

Girls, the Dean of Boys, the respective supervisor, and the ROTC Major wearing his white gloves. I have often wondered if this inspection team was ever really deployed or if this was just a scare tactic to get us to clean our rooms. Whatever, it certainly worked.

- Study hour was held every school night from 7:30–8:30 p.m. We sat at study tables set up in the basement, and our supervisor monitored us as we studied. Homework was to be completed first, and then we could read a book or write. There was no talking or radio.
- Bedtime was now 9:00 p.m.
- Each person was assigned a daily/weekly chore such as cleaning the living room, mopping the halls, or cleaning the bathrooms. This assignment lasted for a month, after which we each received a new assignment with a new room to clean. Most girls were also assigned dining room detail.
- Only black and white shoes were worn in the dining room. Black flats could be worn to church on Sundays and for special occasions. We could also wear non-black and white shoes to school if we owned them, but many girls only owned the state-issued shoes.
- Only dresses or skirts could be worn to school, and they were to be long enough to cover our knees. This rule was relaxed somewhat as shorter styles came into vogue in the late '60s.
- Families could visit once per month, on Saturdays and Sundays from 1:00–5:00 p.m. These visits could be either on or off campus. Children could also leave with family for vacations—two weeks in the summer and from Christmas Day until New Year's Eve. Children, even the youngest in Peter Pan, were not allowed family visits off campus during the first year of residence in the Home.
- Children were not permitted to walk around campus, especially in out-of-bounds areas, without an activity slip or a hospital permission slip approved by our supervisor or a teacher during school hours.
- On weekends, 1:00–3:00 p.m. was quiet time in the cottages. That meant no radios or loud talking. We could sleep, rest, read, or write. This rule was relaxed as we grew older.

Some of the rules were age dependent. I liked knowing what to expect at each new age as I grew. For instance:

Garfield cottage on the girls' campus. This is a typical main campus cottage.

- 13 Years—We could wear lipstick, light eye shadow, and hosiery (panty-hose were not yet a thing). We could join older girls on a Town Pass to go to movies or shopping in Xenia.
- 15 Years and 9th Grade—We could start dating, supervised of course, but still a date. We could attend high school dances.
- 16 Years—We could drink coffee or tea, captain a dining room detail group, and request a Town Pass for Saturday or Sunday afternoons from 1:00–5:00 p.m. During this time we were permitted to walk downtown to Xenia to shop or see a movie, where we could meet our boyfriend. Town passes were first initiated by our supervisor, and then approved by the supervisor of each person named on the pass. Final approval came from the dean of girls (or boys).

One of the most important things we quickly needed to learn was how to get along, both with the other kids and the adults. There were always the "tough" girls, the bullies, who set the tone on campus. If you were deemed to be "weird," not good or tough enough, these girls could make your life miserable. Their bullying was mostly verbal and emotional, not so much physical. It seemed as though many of the other girls followed their lead and acted in

An approved Town Pass for Phyllis, Kathy, and me to shop in Xenia during our senior year.

the same manner both to avoid being bullied themselves and to fit in. I don't believe this was the case for the boys—most of their bullying seemed to be physical. We lived in this environment in our cottages, school and in just about every aspect of our lives; it was hard to escape.

Learning to "fly under the radar" to go unnoticed, a technique I learned in Peter Pan, was invaluable to me on campus in dealing with bullies. Fortunately I found out there were also a lot of nice girls to be friends with.

Looking back, I now realize we were all learning how to live in the Home, how to live with and get along with others, and how to live our lives separated from our families. We all had our own baggage and our own way of coping. I felt sorry for kids who were picked on; I wish I had been kinder to them. I know that many still carry today the emotional scars from that long-ago bullying.

Jeannie was two years ahead of me in school and had many friends who sometimes let me hang around with them, too. Watching these older girls, I learned how to apply makeup, fix my hair (no more ugly bowl cuts for girls on campus!), and dress more stylish. I watched and listened as they played records, and I joined in singing our favorite songs along with radio station WING. I loved these days spent with the older girls. While roommates, Jeannie and I occasionally quarreled as sisters sometimes do. We once had a fight over a hairbrush, and were quickly moved to separate rooms. The following summer Jeannie moved to Garfield B, a cottage for older girls. We never shared a room or cottage again.

In Jackson A, my "supervisor" (no more "Mommy" on campus) was Mrs. Inez Hairopoulos. She was older, a quiet, slow-moving lady. She taught me how to embroider just enough to sew my initials in my clothes rather than using the big, black permanent markers we used in Peter Pan. She also taught me to darn holes in my socks using a light bulb to support the heel of the sock. I didn't realize at the time that she was very sick. She had been my supervisor for a very short time before she died from cancer.

Mrs. Carrie Purtell became my new supervisor. She was a friendly, small, gray-haired (sometimes purplish-haired) lady—strict, but fair. Mrs. Purtell seemed to like to handle discipline herself within the cottage rather than as-signing detention. Her favorite punishment was making us write, for instance:

"I will turn my socks right side out before I put them in the laundry."

The sentences she assigned seemed long to me, and she didn't skimp on the number of times they had to be written. Some of her writing assignments could take an entire weekend's free time. Mrs. Purtell might require I write each sentence 100, 500, 1,000 times, sometimes even more. And the lines were to be written all the way across the page. No cheating by writing in columns. No "I I I, will will will, turn, turn, turn..." If caught, that was grounds for tearing up our paper and starting all over.

After Peter Pan and some of the punishments doled out there, I re-ally didn't mind. I would rather have been outside playing, but this was not a harsh punishment at all, and sometimes seemed almost silly. There were usually several other girls at the table writing, too, and we kept each other company.

Once Mrs. Purtell came on board, we didn't get away with much, as she seemed to notice everything. One day I was outside playing with grasshop-pers. I had prepared a glass jar, filled it with grass, and poked holes in the lid. I caught several grasshoppers and put them in the jar. When it was time to come in from the playground, I hid the jar under a bush so I could play with my grasshopper pets later. I didn't realize I was breaking any rule. Mrs. Purtell caught me, and you can probably guess what happened next.

"I will not catch grasshoppers and put them in a jar."

"I will not catch grasshoppers and put them in a jar."

"I will not catch grasshoppers and put them in a jar."

Lesson learned—I never did that again, and my little pets were set free.

Mrs. Purtell's home was in a little town about an hour away. On her days off, she gave the girls in our cottage turns going home with her for a visit. She started by taking girls who did not have family vacations, but I eventually received a turn. It was a nice little trip, and I met her son and his family. She was the only supervisor I had who spent one-on-one time like this with the girls in her cottage.

One time I whined about never getting any mail. My family visited, but seldom wrote letters to me. When Mrs. Purtell went on a vacation out west, she sent me a post card, and mentioned that she wanted me to receive some mail as the other girls did. I was so thrilled to receive mail that I memorized the little cartoon on the front of the post card. I now realize it was a little bit naughty, but I was too young to comprehend that back then. I also believe that Mrs. Purtell didn't find it off-color in the least, or she would never have sent it to me.

Said the big red rooster to the little red hen, "You haven't laid an egg since the Lord knows when."

Said the little red hen to the big red rooster, "You don't come around as often as you used to."

Each supervisor was given two days off per week. During that time, the main relief supervisor, Mrs. Lois Smith, took her place. Her husband sometimes stayed with her. She was a nice, but no-nonsense lady. When we misbehaved, she would shake her finger at us.

"You've fixed yourself for the weekend." That meant, straighten up or she would put us on detention with no privileges.

Mrs. Smith always wore her white hair in a tight flip rolled at the nape of her neck. We lovingly coined her hairdo "The Smith Roll."

I was in Jackson A for at least four years. The summer before I entered 10th grade I was transferred to an older girls' cottage, Taft A. My new supervisor was Mrs. Alice Bates. Mrs. Bates was a rather large woman, and the older girls in the cottage nicknamed her "Brutus." Mrs. Bates was often cranky, but I sort of liked her. When I think of her, I do remember her grumpiness, but also her beautiful smile, twinkling eyes, and ornery sense of humor when she was around other adults. I think if I had known her after I was grown up, we might have been friends, and I think she would have been a lot of fun to be around. I also remember, though, that when she had it in for you, there seemed to be no way out. Her punishment of choice was not writing, but detention.

Expectations and responsibilities increased as we progressed through the cottage levels. In Taft A bedtime was 9:30 p.m. We were now responsible for our own laundry. We had an old wringer washing machine, and we hung our clothes to dry on a clothesline in the basement. It was important that we start our laundry by washing whites first and ending with our darkest colors, because each girl used the same water for all her clothing. After the clothes were dry, we used a soda bottle with a sprinkler cap to dampen the clothes to be ironed. They were then rolled up and placed in a plastic bag until we ironed them. All of our laundry had to be washed, ironed and put away by the end of the day on Thursday. If not, we were placed on detention. This could pose a challenge because there were only two or three washing machines and a few irons. It was sometimes hard to get a turn. Older girls always seemed to have first dibs on the irons. No excuses; detention if our laundry wasn't finished.

Detention could be imposed for any infraction of any rule such as a dirty room, chores not done correctly, homework not completed (yes, the teachers were in cahoots with the supervisors), or misbehaving anywhere on campus. A detention list was distributed on Friday afternoons. Any girl who had been placed on detention had no privileges for a week. That meant no Saturday evening movie, no sporting events, no weekend activities, and no dances; we were cottage-bound for that entire week.

Each week, a different cottage was assigned as the detention cottage. During the Saturday evening movie, girls from all over campus who were on detention gathered in the basement of the detention cottage to spend the evening studying or reading in silence. The supervisor of that cottage sat with the girls and maintained quiet and order until the movie was over. I remember being on detention only a few times. Some of the detention supervisors were kind and gave us snacks such as popcorn, candy or cookies. Others were there to be sure we studied every single minute.

Supervisors could also assign fatigue as the punishment for more minor infractions of rules. Fatigue meant doing extra chores such as washing windows or walls, waxing floors, or any other chores the supervisor assigned.

Girls on dining room detail were placed on fatigue rather than detention for any infraction of detail rules. The captain and dining room supervisors imposed this punishment for arriving late or for not properly completing required assignments. Fatigue was usually served in the dining room on Saturday mornings. The fatigue assignments could be mopping floors, scrubbing counters, tables and chairs, folding napkins, filling salt and pepper shakers, or any myriad of assignments doled out by the dining room staff.

The most serious punishment of all was reserved for those children who ran away or caused serious property damage. They were placed in isolation rooms in the hospital with no visitors and sometimes no clothes. They stayed in these rooms for a predetermined length of time. The only punishment worse than isolation was to be sent away. There was a constant looming threat of being sent to Juvenile Detention for those children who continually misbehaved or ran away.

Life in Taft A was fun for me. Days were filled with friends, school, homework, piano practice, dining room detail, laundry, sporting events, and thinking about boys. I loved hanging out with some of the older girls in my cottage. I watched and learned as they applied makeup and got ready for dates. One of the girls always wrote down on her calendar what outfit she was wearing for each date to ensure that she didn't wear the same one twice in a row. Some of these girls were also extremely good students and challenged me to do my best in school, too.

I loved to sneak quietly down to the basement first thing in the morning.

I experienced my first best friend in Taft A. Joanne was my age, in all my classes, and we became dear friends. We shared our deepest secrets and our clothes, although we really weren't allowed to wear another girl's clothing. I cherished our friendship. My roommate Betsy was a year younger than me, and was Jerry's first real girlfriend. We became good friends as well.

Once or twice each year, the campus cottages held their own "Cottage Party." These could be gym and swim events where we played volleyball, basketball, jumped on the trampoline and swam in the pool. Depending on the age group, each student could invite a special friend or a boyfriend. Refreshments of pop and potato chips were usually served. Sometimes the supervisor would furnish cookies or other snacks, too. Another popular cottage party was staying at the cottage and inviting a date or special friend for an evening of dancing, watching television, eating junk food, or playing games. We all looked forward to our special cottage parties. One of my favorite cottage party invitations was for a dance in my boyfriend Skip's cottage while we were dating.

Two of my campus cottages had cockroaches. While that sounds disgusting to me today, back then I thought it was pretty cool. I only ever saw them in the basement, never upstairs in our rooms. Exterminators came around quite often, but those little buggers always seemed to return. I loved to sneak quietly down to the basement first thing in the morning, flip on the lights, and watch the many, many cockroaches scatter.

In Taft A, Mrs. Bates allowed us to keep a small pet like a hamster or guinea pig in a little cage. I opted for two little white mice. While I wouldn't touch one today, back then I enjoyed playing with my little guys.

The summer before starting my senior year, I moved to Hayes Hall, the senior girls' cottage. My supervisor was Mrs. Wanda Quickle. She was brand new to the Home and stayed only for that one year. She was a friendly older lady with gray hair, a wonderful smile, and she loved to wear pretty, bright, perky hats. I felt she took a personal interest in each of us as she inquired about our dates and activities in a loving and receptive way, much as I imagined a mother would. I don't remember ever receiving any punishment at all while Mrs. Quickle was my supervisor. She seemed to share our excitement as we prepared for prom and graduation day. She joined in on the fun and laughter as we all gathered around the television on Monday evenings to watch *Laugh-In*, the most popular show that year.

Campus life was completely different for senior girls than for younger girls. Rules were much more relaxed as we were given more and more autonomy. Bedtime was 10:00 p.m. as a general rule, but it was never strongly enforced. In order to better prepare us for life on our own, we fixed our own breakfast and dinner in the cottage, and went to the main dining room only for lunch. Senior girls were no longer assigned to dining room detail.

I had a harder time getting up in the morning knowing I didn't have to go to the dining room for breakfast anymore. I usually ignored the 6:20 a.m. whistle, and Mrs. Quickle let me sleep in until the 6:40 a.m. whistle. Such luxury and kindness!

We senior girls took turns planning menus and cooking dinners. Mrs. Quickle helped us order from the main kitchen the food supplies that we would need for our weekly menus. She also fixed breakfast for us most mornings. She was a great cook, and helped us learn to prepare some fantastic meals. We made pork chops, chicken, roast beef and stew, as well as cookies, pies and cakes. She helped me experiment to make my grandma's potpie recipe. We ate well in Hayes Hall.

When I moved to Hayes Hall A, I felt lucky to have a room to myself. But in late August shortly before school started, a new senior girl entered the Home. Kathy was assigned to be my roommate. She was a nice girl, and we soon became good friends. Phyllis lived just down the hall and also became a good friend. The three of us ran around together most of the time. My friend Joanne lived on the other side of Hayes Hall, and we remained friends. Joanne, Kathy, Phyllis and I were all about the same size, and we four girls shared our clothes. This quadrupled the size of our wardrobes, and I enjoyed wearing their cool outfits. One of the worst things about graduating and leaving the Home was downsizing to just my own small wardrobe.

Orphan Slang

"Slang is a language that rolls up its sleeves,
spits on its hands and goes to work." –Carl Sandburg

We Home kids lived together, ate together, went to school together, and we developed our own "Orphan Slang."

Abbreviations and words peculiar to the Home:

Clodhoppers—Our state-issued black and white saddle shoes.

The Corner—The corner between the school and trades buildings where boys could walk with girls and share a little kiss; usually after a dance or activity; and always well chaperoned by a dean, chaplain or principal.

CQ—Call to Quarters; time to come in from the playground.

Detail—Dining room chore/assignment

Junior Campus—Cottages for children too old for Peter Pan and too young to live on the main campus; usually 9–11-year-old children lived here.

Main Campus—Cottages for older children; usually 12 years and older.

Mommy—Supervisor in Peter Pan; i.e., Mommy Carmen

Monkey Suits—Coveralls sometimes worn by little children in Peter Pan.

Newkies—New kids

OD—Officer of the Day—A student ROTC officer assigned each day, stationed at the Main Building as a constable to maintain peace, assist employees with unruly kids, and provide security. They raised and lowered the flag each day. Known by his armband with the letters "OD."

Orfenz Den or Den—Our weekend hangout and dance hall.

Orphans—Our term of endearment for each other; Who we were, not What we were!

OSSO Home—A common abbreviation for the Ohio Soldiers' and Sailors' Orphans' Home.

Peter Pan—The building that housed the youngest children, under age ten.

Rev—Our term of endearment for our Chaplain.

Sarge—Our term of endearment for the Sergeant in charge of ROTC.

Supervisors/Houseparents—The women (mostly) in charge of the cottages

"The Home"—The Ohio Soldiers' and Sailors' Orphans' Home.

Your People—Your family outside of the Home. For example, "Your People have arrived." Or, "I can't wait until My People arrive."

Our Slang Vocabulary:

Batchie—Bathroom, John, Potty, Latrine

Buck—I already knew that; stale news

Burr—Boy's haircut, usually way too short.

Cheese it—Stop talking, here comes an adult

Dag/Dag Man—Gosh or darn it

Doormat—When your boyfriend (or girlfriend) controls you, walks all over you; or takes advantage of you, and when you spend all your free time with or thinking about your boyfriend (or girlfriend)—you're a doormat.

Drill—ROTC Training

Fag—Cigarette—"Can I borrow a fag?"

Fake out—"Not really," or "Just joking."

Flick—Skip class (very rare in the Home)

Follow you—"I get the next puff on that cigarette."

Going down—Getting out of the hospital and back to the cottage.

Going over the hill—Going to the Gate Store; usually for buying cigarettes.

Going with someone—Dating someone

Got a log?—Got a cigarette?

Gutchies—Underwear

Heaterator—Our term for radiator. We called the steam heating pipes in our cottages heaterators.

Next man in—Gets the shower next

Nutcracker—The best sledding hill in Ohio.

Promenade—Walking with your boyfriend (or girlfriend) on Sunday afternoons around the parade field.

Quit someone—Break up or stop dating someone

Seater—Peter Pan word for rear end; I hated getting my seater spanked.

Seats back—"Don't you dare take my seat while I'm gone!"

Slop—Our food, even though it was usually pretty good.

Slop cans—Where we dumped food to be sent to the pigs at the Farm.

Speaks—First bid on something

Sponge or sponging—Borrowing, with or without asking first

Square—Not cool, weird

State property—Wards of the state. "Can't touch us, we're state property."

Sucks—Tattletales

Tennies—Tennis shoes

Tough—Cute adjective reserved for guys; "he's tough"

Vago—Vacation, time spent away from the Home with family.

Play Time

"Play is the work of childhood" —Jean Piaget

One advantage of growing up in the Home was that I could always find someone to play with. In Peter Pan, each cottage had a playroom where we spent our free time, especially in the winter.

My Aunt Loualtha made sure Jeannie and I had several dolls. I loved playing with them, and kept them in my toy chest. While in Peter Pan, I begged and begged her for a real bride doll. Loualtha said she thought I was too young for a doll such as that, but eventually she relented and bought one for me. Oh, how I loved my dolls! Not everyone had family to buy them dolls, and I was required to share mine. When one of the older girls pulled all the hair out of my new bride doll's head, I was devastated. I knew Loualtha would not be happy, and I didn't want to tell her.

"My new bride doll is ruined," I hesitantly relayed the news to Loualtha at her next visit. I showed her my now bald and no longer beautiful doll.

I was right. Loualtha was not happy at all, especially since she had given in after telling me that I was too young for such a doll. "That's the last doll I will

Me holding my doll baby in front of a toy chest in the Pan 6 playroom.

ever give you," she threatened. But one Christmas when I was a little older and no longer had to share my dolls, Loualtha got me and Jeannie matching dolls dressed in red plaid skirts with white blouses. She also bought each of us an outfit that matched our doll.

When the weather was decent we played outside on the playground. The Peter Pan girls' playground had a merry-go-round, swing set, sliding board, sand box, and monkey bars that provided hours of entertainment.

The playground at Taylor B, my junior campus cottage, had just a swing set, but we could walk over to the Peter Pan playground and play with the younger children there. The Taylor cottages were close to the farm, and Mommy Carmen often took us on long walks there to see the cows and pigs and the various vegetables being grown. We usually ended our walk by stopping at the apple orchard where each girl picked her own apple to eat on the walk home.

Mowing crews kept the grass all over campus trimmed and beautiful, but during the summer it was hard for them to keep up, and the grass could get pretty high. When it was mowed, the grass clippings were just left on the ground to dry out. I loved to take the grass clippings to form an outline of an imaginary house. My houses were usually about 10' x 10.' I painstakingly laid out the living room, kitchen, bedrooms, and bathroom. As other girls joined the fun, we were able to lay out a small neighborhood. But alas, wind, rain, the mowing crew or mean kids came along and we would have to start all over, making our houses just a little better each time.

My first cottage on the main campus was Jackson, where there was no longer a dedicated playroom. We went outside to play during most of our free time. Our playground now had two large swing sets, a sliding board, tether ball, volleyball court, four-square court, a softball field as well as a lot of grassy space. Each cottage had a large veranda that extended over the first-story living room. Jackson A's veranda was right beside our playground. We were never allowed to go out on the veranda for fear we would get hurt, but we Jackson A girls did it anyway. It was a great spot for sunbathing and also a good place for daredevil jumping because it was only one story high. We just had to be careful to not get caught, and luckily I never did.

The first new game I learned upon moving to Jackson A was "jacks." It seemed that all the older girls played and most of them were really good. I got pretty good at this game, too. Another favorite game was Monopoly, a game we played both indoors as well as outside on the playground.

When I was in the 5th or 6th grade, Loualtha and Joe bought the four of us each a bike. I was allowed to keep mine as long as I shared with the other girls when I wasn't using it. The Home also had some bikes available. I remember riding only in the evenings after supper on a road that wound past the girls' playground. Round and round we rode all evening long.

Miss Whilding was our playground supervisor as well as Physical Education teacher. She organized and refereed volleyball games, but as interest seemed to dwindle, she taught us a new game, "four-square." This became my favorite game, and I played it whenever there were girls willing to play. We used the asphalt volleyball court. Eventually this game became so popular that the volleyball nets and posts were completely removed and lines were painted for four-square. Miss Whilding often played, too, as a long line of waiting girls formed and wound completely around the court.

During the summer evenings, Miss Whilding organized intramural softball games between the girls' cottages. I loved to play third base whenever I was picked for the team. Whether playing or cheering for my cottage team, these games were the most fun to be had on a long summer evening.

Some evenings I would see Rev. Howard leaving his office after working a little late. My friends and I would beg him to take us for ice cream at Betty & Bob's, the local ice cream stand in Xenia. His answer was usually, "OK, let's get ice cream." Rev. Howard was the best!

While the girls spent their long summer days on the playground, boys on main campus were assigned to the Summer Work Program. They were assigned to work crews to pick up paper, paint around campus, weld and repair, trim trees, shrubbery and weeds, sickle the creek bank, make cottage repairs, work on the farm, and even clean cabins for summer use at the Home's camp. The days were usually long and hot, and some of the jobs were definitely better than others. Some of the boys signed up for summer school as an excuse to avoid this work program. I am not sure why the girls were not also assigned to summer work crews, and can only imagine that it would have interfered with our scheduled dining room chores. I would have welcomed the opportunity to have something more substantial to do than go outside on the playground every morning, afternoon and evening in the summer.

Me as a teenager on the swing set near Jackson A on the main campus.

Each summer, all of us Home kids attended the Greene County Fair in Xenia. Each girl was given a pair of either blue or red plaid pedal pushers (similar to today's capris), with either a red or blue striped t-shirt. The boys were also given matching t-shirts, so all of us were dressed quite similarly as we enjoyed this special day. I'm sure our clothing made it easier for the adults to keep track of us in the crowds. We were given three tickets for rides at the fair, and we could purchase additional tickets for five cents each. I tried to save my allowance to buy as many ride tickets as I could. Younger children stayed in cottage groups with their supervisors while older children were free to go off and enjoy the fair with their friends. When I dated Skip, he had saved every penny of his allowance for a couple months in order to buy tickets, and we were able to ride together all afternoon thanks to his thriftiness. I have fond memories of secret kisses at the top of the Ferris wheel and sharing a caramel apple before we returned to the Home.

The Orfenz Den was a large recreation area in the basement of the Auditorium. It was open to students on Saturday and Sunday afternoons as well as a couple evenings during the week. Main campus students in grades 8 and below could attend for an hour, and then grades 9 and above could attend for the next hour. Students could just "hang out," visit, play ping pong, or watch television. When I had money, I usually bought a bag of barbecue potato chips and a can of Coke. Going to the Den was a good opportunity to visit with your boyfriend without having an official date.

One summer evening, Ms. Henize, Dean of Girls, sent out invitations to all the girls on campus to attend a "Come as You Are Party" in the Orfenz Den—right now! Girls arrived in bathrobes, pajamas, pedal pushers, hair in

This is the same location near Jackson A, but today the swing set is gone. I'm surrounded by some of my family, my daughter, Heidi, some of my grandchildren, and some of Jeannie's grandchildren.

curlers, whatever they were wearing at the moment. We enjoyed a couple hours of dancing, television, ping pong, and just hanging out. Although it was great fun, I remember having this type of party only that one time.

The swimming pool was located in the basement of the gymnasium. It was often open on weekend afternoons for open swims. Most of the time these open swims were "boys only" or "girls only," but occasionally there were mixed swims for older students. I usually swam with my girlfriends Phyllis and Kathy, and we were often joined by several boys from our class. We made a game of throwing pennies or whatever change we could find into the deep end of the pool and then diving for the money. We also swam races and had fun diving. Open swims were always much more fun when the boys could join us.

While in 5th through 7th grades, roller skating was one of my favorite activities. We skated both in the basement as well as outside on the playground sidewalks, using adjustable metal clip-on skates that fit right over our shoes. We were sometimes allowed to skate on Friday evenings in the Armory with the boys, chaperoned by teacher volunteers. Around the same time, we were often driven downtown to the Xenia Skating Rink on Saturday and Sunday afternoons for several hours of indoor skating. I don't remember who sponsored these afternoons of fun, but I was always eager to participate.

Sledding was our most popular winter sport. Near the power house on the boys' side, there was a large hill popularly referred to as "The Nutcracker." We didn't have many real sleds so we used whatever we could find to slide down this big hill. I remember sliding on a flattened cardboard box. Plastic bags were also a popular option. I'm positive the boys were able to come up with many other makeshift ideas for sleds. One year the Home Advisory Committee sponsored a snow party with sledding, snowballing, snowmen, and just playing in the snow. They provided hot chocolate, kindly served to us kids by the kitchen staff. We loved snow!

With all the various activities offered at the Home, it was hard to stay bored for long.

Camp Cooper

"Kellie, kellie, kellie, kellie, wash, wash, wash, wash,
Kee-a, kee-a, kiy-a.
Oh hail to thee, Camp Cooper, Our hearts are ever true to thee."
—Home girls on the bus headed for Camp

Camp Cooper holds a special place in my heart, and I feel sure it holds that same special place in the hearts of most Home kids. One of my favorite summer experiences was spending a week or two at Camp Cooper. Weekly camp schedules were rotated between boys and girls so each child on main campus had a chance to go to camp at least once each summer. Students in band had their own special week of fun and practice at Camp Cooper. Some of the younger boys were always sent to camp during the yearly Association of Ex-Pupils Reunion the first weekend in July. This ensured that their rooms on campus were available for use by the visiting former Home kids.

Camp Cooper was owned by the Home and was named after Myers Y. Cooper, a former Governor of Ohio. It was near Clifton, Ohio, about a half-hour drive from the Home, and was situated on the top of a ridge overlooking the Little Miami River Gorge. Mr. and Mrs. Coulter were the residential caretakers. Mrs. Coulter cooked and served all the meals while Mr. Coulter managed all the other requirements of the camp.

Six cabins filled with bunk beds were each able to accommodate ten to twelve people. The girls' camp director who was also our Physical Education teacher, Miss Whilding, stayed in a 7th cabin. The camp encompassed approximately 10 acres and included a softball field, mess hall, showers, shelter house, latrine, tether ball, and both horseshoe and quoit pits. There was no swimming pool, but arrangements were made for us Home campers to swim in the Orton Pool at nearby John Bryant State Park. We swam there during the morning hours before the park opened while the water was still icy cold, not yet warmed by the afternoon sun. The park was a half-hour walk

Camp Cooper cabins 1, 2, and 3—closest to the Little Miami River gorge.

through the gorge on beautiful hiking trails that included some rock climbing. I loved the hike to the pool as much as I loved swimming.

Once we arrived at camp we were given our cabin assignment. Each cabin was assigned a counselor, an older high school girl. Our counselor was responsible for all our daily activities, from getting up and dressing in the morning, to being on time at the mess hall, to settling down in the evening. When I reached 10th or 11th grade, I got my turn at being counselor.

The cabins each held five or six bunk beds. The oldest girls got their first choice of the beds, and so they usually took the bottom bunks, leaving the top bunks for the youngest girls. Though we were not allowed to write on the cabin walls, they were covered with names, years, hearts, and sometimes naughty little poems and sayings, that could only be seen from the top bunks.

Each morning after breakfast, we cleaned our cabins from top to bottom, ready for Miss Whilding's daily inspection. We worked hard to be sure we had gotten rid of every single cobweb and any dirt on the floor and porch. We were also assigned turns cleaning the shelter house, latrine, dining hall, and showers. The only latrine was used by both boys and girls during their separate camping weeks. It was full of daddy longlegs spiders, so cleaning duty there was not so much fun. The boys, I assumed, wrote silly, sometimes naughty, graffiti on the walls of the latrine for our reading pleasure.

"Here I sit all broken hearted...."

"All turds over three pounds must be lowered by hand." That always made me curious about boys and their pooping abilities.

When I first started going to camp, there was no shower. We used the sinks in the latrine to wash up, and showered off after swimming at John Bryant State Park. A shower room was finally built, but provided only cold water and zero privacy. None of us lingered for long; it was freezing. And that pesky little crop-duster airplane that was circling overhead—we were sure the pilot could see us in that roofless little shower house.

Each day our counselor, with input from all of the girls in the cabin, determined the day's activities. We could choose between half-day or full-day activities. The shorter, half-day activities could consist of riding bikes, playing in the Little Miami River, hiking in the gorge, or hiking to the little village of Clifton. These were all great fun. We played in the river at our special spot, always getting wet and dirty.

The beautiful gorge was filled with trees, birds, animal sounds, moss-covered rocks and ledges, and paths interrupted by large tree roots. When hiking in the gorge we looked for our favorite landmarks: Devil's Crack, Blue Hole, Steamboat Rock, and Turtle Rock. The boys sometimes camped overnight in the gorge near Blue Hole, something the girls never did, nor, would they have wanted to. I certainly never wanted that experience! We were always on the lookout for "George d'Gorge," a part-human and part-animal creature who lived in the gorge. I never saw him; I think he came out only at night to scare little kids who didn't belong in his gorge. During the day, however, I enjoyed the short hike through the gorge to nearby Clifton, where we stopped to visit a black bear that was held in a cage near the grocery store.

We could also choose to take one or two all-day hikes each week to Xenia, Yellow Springs or Cedarville. When a cabin group chose an all-day hike, Mrs. Coulter packed sack lunches to take along. My favorite all-day hike was to Xenia. It was a long, hot walk on asphalt roads surrounded by tall corn fields much of the way. The asphalt beneath our feet got so hot from the sun that it formed bubbles. I had fun stepping on the bubbles as I walked along, listening to the merry popping sound each made. Whenever a car was approaching, the counselor would call out almost as a chant, "Heads up and over" which always reminded me of "Red rover, red rover." There was not much traffic on these roads, and when a car did approach us, it was usually Miss Whilding making sure we were all ok. Her days must have been spent checking up on all the cabin groups as we ventured out in several different directions.

We sang songs as we hiked along. A few that I still remember were:
Gee Mom I Want to Go Home
I Don't Know but I've Heard Rumors
The Ants Go Marching One By One
My Hillbilly Will

At some point we would run out of songs, and seemed to finish almost every hike with, *One Hundred Bottles of Beer on the Wall*. That was good for probably a half-mile or so. We all knew where we could stop to ask for water. We never passed up that one friendly farmhouse that not only provided water from their hose, but also set out paper cups for our use.

Once we arrived at our Xenia stop, a little mom and pop grocery store, we bought drinks to go with our lunches. Jeannie was sometimes in my cabin and she introduced me to the ritual of buying a bottle of RC Cola at this store. That was the only place I had ever had RC Cola, and it was a special treat reserved for this Xenia hike. We then sat on a little grassy hill outside of that store to rest, eat our lunch and drink our RCs before returning to camp.

We began each meal at Camp Cooper by singing a prayer. For breakfast we sang:

God has created a new day
Silver and green and gold.
Hopes that the sunset will find us
Worthy his gifts to hold.

Our song at lunch:

For health and strength and daily food
We praise thy name, oh Lord.
Amen

Camp Cooper shelter house and cabins 6 and 7.

We sang for our supper, too.

Evening is here
The board is spread
Thanks be to God
Who gives us bread.

Mrs. Coulter's meals were outstanding, with her specialty being dessert. She baked wonderful pies, cakes and cookies. Her breakfast toast was also outstanding—it was baked rather than toasted. Crunchy, hot, delicious. Right before bedtime, we all met in the dining hall for a bedtime snack. That was a special treat because we never had bedtime snacks at the Home. Mrs. Coulter often served homemade cookies with the coldest milk I've ever had. It was so cold it contained ice crystals. We all loved it.

Each evening after dinner we played softball until dark. As dusk began to fall and the ball was getting harder to see, Miss Whilding chose two or three of the youngest, newest campers to go turn on the lights to the softball field. I took my turn my first year at camp. I looked everywhere but just couldn't find the switch. I finally shuffled back to the game feeling dejected and embarrassed. By then it was getting really dark, and I had to report that I couldn't find the light switch. Everyone laughed and laughed because there are no lights at the softball field. I watched this scene repeated every time I attended camp, but after that first time I was happy to be in on the joke and able to laugh along with the older girls.

After the softball game, all of the campers gathered at the shelter house for the evening's in-the-dark activities. The ones I remember best were:

- Tin Can Johnny (our own game of kick-the-can)
- Night hikes in the gorge
- Treasure hunts
- Scavenger hunts

For the last night, each cabin made up a skit to perform for the entire camp. We spent much of our free time and hiking time trying to come up with the perfect skit to entertain the group. Everyone in the cabin participated. One of my favorite skits was when one of the cabins placed a large box on the floor at the front of the shelter house. Girls from all the other cabins sat on the floor in front of the box. The box was placed so that we couldn't see inside of it. Whatever was thrown into the box came out three or four times as large. For instance, they threw in a little stick, and pulled a big log out of the box. Next, one of the girls spit into the box, and a stream of water from a hose got those of us on the floor all wet. The last thing thrown in was a little baby doll, and from behind us came that cabin's counselor dressed in a diaper, t-shirt, bonnet, and sporting a pacifier. There were lots of laughs from that little skit.

Miss Whilding put a lot of thought and effort into both the treasure hunt and scavenger hunt. She hid little poems with hints that led us all over camp to the final destination of the treasure hunt. It was very well done and so much fun. For the scavenger hunt, she distributed a list of items to be found and collected around camp. The first cabin that collected all the items on the list was the winner. My first year at camp, the last item on our list was a "whippersnapper." Our counselor grabbed me, said "You'll do!" and we won.

Assocation of Ex-Pupils (AXP) Annual Reunion

"Where Friends and Memories Meet." –AXP Slogan

Former students of the Home, ex-pupils, gathered at the Home the first weekend in July each year. This 3-day event began on Friday morning and ended after lunch on Sunday. For the nominal price of an AXP membership, ex-pupils were invited to stay on campus, sleep in the cottages, and eat every meal with the children in the dining room.

An air of excitement overtook the campus as preparations began for the arrival of this large group. We cleaned our cottages from top to bottom. We washed windows, re-waxed and polished hallway floors, and swept the porches in addition to our normal weekly cleaning assignments. Girls with rooms on the ground floor temporarily moved upstairs for the weekend so their rooms could be used by ex-pupils. Some of the younger boys on campus were sent to Camp Cooper so their entire cottages could be used to house ex-pupils. A large tent placed on the parade field covered the many tables and chairs set underneath to provide a comfortable visiting place for the visitors. A concession stand was placed outside of the Main Building. All the grounds, newly mowed and manicured, looked especially beautiful and inviting. A large "Welcome Home" sign was placed just inside the main entrance gate.

Finally, it was time and folks started arriving. The cottages rapidly filled with returning students and their families. While I lived in Jackson A, a family from Indiana always stayed in our cottage. They had a little girl, Mary Ellen, who was about three years old. We girls were thrilled to watch, play and maybe even fight over her from time to time so her parents could enjoy visiting with their friends. Mary Ellen still returns to Reunion each year and it's always a treat to see her again.

While most of the activities were for the enjoyment of the ex-pupils, we students were included in some events. A group of ex-pupils joined the boys at Camp Cooper for Bingo, where prizes were awarded to the winners. On the Home grounds, ex-pupils played games with the Peter Pan and junior campus children. A couple of softball games were played between ex-pupils and students. One game was Home girls against middle aged ex-pupil men. The men were required to bat left-handed and throw left-handed. Another game was Home boys against ex-pupils. Even when I didn't play, it was fun to watch and cheer.

Mr. McKinley Warth, an older ex-pupil, brought his camera to every Reunion to take pictures of the Home children. He concentrated most of his efforts on taking pictures of Peter Pan children. He then developed the pictures and returned them to the children or the administration. These are the only childhood pictures some of us kids ever owned. Today a couple of extremely dedicated ex-pupils have turned these pictures into digital format and they are posted on the Home's Facebook picture page for all of us to enjoy. I'm forever grateful to Mr. Warth for his kindness and foresight, knowing how much these pictures would be treasured someday.

The Home band played *Reveille* on the two Reunion mornings. I'm not sure if the whistle also blew those mornings, but *Reveille* was a pleasant wake-up call for both the kids and the ex-pupils. The band sometimes performed in concert during Reunion. Some of the ex-pupils enjoyed joining the band for these events.

A banquet was held on Saturday evening in the dining room. Many of the ex-pupils dressed in their finest evening apparel. The banquet was usually the best meal served all year. Luckily, we children were served the same delicious food. The menus were varied over the years, but I especially remember roast beef and mashed potatoes with gravy because that was my favorite meal.

The final day of Reunion made me a little bit sad as I watched the ex-pupils pack their bags and drive away. There was such a pleasant, festive air during the three days, but it all faded away as things returned to normal on campus.

Today our AXP still holds a three-day Reunion on the weekend closest to the 4th of July, but things have definitely changed since the Home closed. Dayton Christian Schools purchased the school buildings, auditorium and gymnasium, and they now operate a fully functioning private school on our Home grounds. The Christian organization, Athletes in Action (AIA), has purchased the remainder of the Home grounds. Many buildings are now

Janice and Jeannie taken at an AXP Reunion by ex-pupil McKinley Warth. For many children, Mr. Warth's pictures were the only ones they have from their childhood.

gone: Peter Pan, junior campus cottages, Five campus cottage buildings, the hospital, armory, superintendent's residence, employee residences, band shell, farm and laundry. While not our old Home, AIA has made many positive changes. The dining room has been updated to a modern, functioning banquet hall. The hospital land is now an assisted living area. The superintendent's home and football field make up a vibrant senior citizens' community. The remaining cottages have been totally renovated and now include air conditioning and restrooms in each room.

Several of these renovated rooms are available to ex-pupils for a fee during Reunion. Most ex-pupils stay in nearby hotels. Reunion meals are served picnic style. The usual breakfast fare is coffee and donuts, followed by hot dogs and hamburgers for lunch and dinner. At a recent Reunion the menu was changed up a bit with sausage and eggs for breakfast and a pig roast for dinner. Some extremely dedicated ex-pupils man the grills and serve the meals. The Saturday evening banquet has been held at various local venues. At the last Reunion I attended, Board members planned, cooked and served the banquet in the Orfenz Den.

Because the Home permanently closed in 1995, there have been no new ex-pupil members, and our membership has declined steadily since that date. We have begun accepting children of ex-pupils and former employees into our membership, and allowing them to hold positions on the AXP Board. With these changes, membership has started to increase. The ex-pupils still meet throughout the year for Memorial Day, Halloween and Christmas. Smaller local groups meet often for breakfast or dinner.

There are no longer Home children to enjoy Bingo or softball with the ex-pupils. I miss the noise and joy the Home children added to our old Reunions. I feel as though we are a group of former orphans wanting to give back, wanting to support our orphanage, but we no longer have an orphanage to support.

Opportunities to Earn Money

*"When done with heart, commitment and integrity,
every job is equally important." –Yolanda Hadid*

I was sixteen that summer when Ms. Henize, the Dean of Girls, called me to her office. I joined a group of about twenty boys and girls assembled outside of her office. She ushered us into a nearby conference room where she explained that the daughter of one of the Home's Trustees was getting married, and had requested that Home students be hired to serve at the wedding.

It was quite an honor to be chosen to help at events like this. Jerry was also in the group, and we were excited to be given this opportunity to earn money. Before we could work this gig, we had to apply for and receive a Social Security card. We would be paid minimum wage which was $1.40 per hour, but I don't remember how much money I made that day.

It was the mid '60s. Dr. Mary Lee, the Board Member, was a well-known physician in Xenia. She was a beautiful light-skinned black woman. This group of twenty teenagers was bussed to Dr. Lee's home. We were each dressed in our Memorial Day outfits of white skirts and blouses with black and white saddle shoes for the girls. The boys wore white pants, white collared but-toned-down shirts, and black shoes.

I felt as though I were stepping into a fairy tale wedding. The bride was beautiful in her exquisite white lace gown. I had never seen anyone so gorgeous in my life. I was also quite impressed with Dr. Lee's elegant home and lawn. We teens passed out appetizers—I especially remember the caviar and champagne. We also served dinner featuring the largest, most succulent steaks I had ever seen.

Dinner was provided for us servers, too. We were invited into the kitchen for hot dogs and chips. We enjoyed our hot dogs, but looked longingly at those steaks. As we cleared the plates off the tables, I noticed that some of the steaks were barely touched, and couldn't help myself. I joined others as we sneaked bites of those steaks. They were amazingly good.

While I was in the kitchen with Jerry, a boy I didn't know well came over to us with a sample of caviar he had sneaked off the table. We gave it a try, and I thought it was horrible. We later were able to try the champagne, too. I wasn't impressed with that either. However, I was definitely impressed with the caviar thief, whom I dated for several years after this event.

Looking back, the only thing about this wedding that gave me pause was the fact that the groom was not black, but rather Japanese. The bride had about the same skin tone as he had, but I had been taught we should marry only people of the same race. Today I think about how unusual, given the political climate of the 60s, it must have been for these mostly white teenagers to serve at a black wedding. But I never gave it a thought back then. I thought it more bizarre that some of these rich, fancy, well-dressed people barely touched their mouthwatering steaks.

Several Home employees lived in houses on campus, and hired older Home girls to clean their houses on Saturdays. Over a two-year period during my sophomore and junior years, I spent many Saturday mornings cleaning Rev. Howard's house for $5.00 each week. Another girl worked with me, and we alternated weeks between cleaning the bathroom and ironing. Rev. Howard had two teenage sons. I became friends with his son, Mick. Chatting with him made the time seem to fly, and I looked forward to those Saturday morning chores.

Any money made doing jobs like this was taken and held in the Dean's office to use for specific larger purchases. I saved mine to use around graduation time for special clothes and senior pictures.

During the annual July AXP Reunion, all the high school girls were required to serve in the dining room at each meal over the three days. A tip jar was set up, and all the tips from all three days were divided among us. We each usually received about $10.00, and were permitted to keep this money. As high school students, we used this money for trips downtown to buy makeup, hosiery, perfume, or jewelry. Older girls were also permitted to go downtown to the movies on Saturday and Sunday afternoons, and this money paid our admission.

Summer Vacation and Family Visits

"Sometimes you will never know the value of a moment until it becomes a memory." –Dr. Seuss

August at last! I loved August because it meant vacation time. Every single year without fail, Loualtha and Joe invited us to their home for at least two weeks. My siblings and I were fortunate to have relatives who were able to take us home both in the summer and at Christmas. There were many children at the Home who never went on a vacation with their family. I felt sadness for those kids. I'm not sure why my family always vacationed in August. I believe it started off that way because we entered the Home on August 14th, and our first vacation started exactly one year later. In later years, we waited until Rick and Jerry were finished with their summer band schedule. I liked the fact that by the time we returned from vacation it was almost time for school to start. School days were definitely more fun for me than long summer breaks.

Loualtha always drove as Joe's eyesight was failing. The car ride to their home in Barberton, Ohio, seemed awfully long. Until I was in high school there were no freeways, so we shared two-lane highways with the semi-trucks for the entire trip. In later years after Interstate 71 was built, Loualtha was hesitant to use it for more than about a third of the trip. She told me that she worried about driving at those high speeds for long distances, that it couldn't be safe. Today I can make that almost eight-hour trip in just over three hours.

"How much longer 'til we get there?" we asked over and over. We took many breaks along the way, stopping for potty, lunch, and ice cream treats. But we still wondered how much longer. Joe sometimes moved to the back seat to play games with us kids. He taught us to play poker, always calling deuces, tres, and one-eyed jacks wild. Every time we passed a particular road sign, "Cleve-Mass Rd," short for Cleveland-Massillon Road, he would laugh

Returning from a summer vacation—Jerry's sad face says it all. We all dreaded our return to the Home after our family visits.

and say, "I've heard of high mass and I've heard of low mass, but I've never heard of Cleve mass." I always looked so forward to that sign just to hear him say it again. Plus, it was only two exits before our exit, so we were almost home.

During our vacation visits, I felt as though we were almost a normal family. Loualtha and Joe made our visits special with dining out, family reunions, swimming, picnics, riding bikes, and just playing like regular kids. At least once during those two weeks they treated us to dinner at a nice, dress-up restaurant where we could order anything on the menu. I didn't know about steak yet, and usually ordered fried chicken. Rick and Joe sometimes ordered frog legs. They always offered to give the rest of us a bite, and each time they were promptly turned down. The Medina County Fair always seemed to be going on during our vacations, and we all went every year. We loved to ride the rides and eat the good carnival food. Loualtha and Joe bought passes for us to swim at local swimming pools or lakes, and we went swimming as often as we could. We all four made friends with children in the neighborhood, and had fun playing with them.

One of Loualtha and Joe's neighbors had four children close to our ages. I was twelve or thirteen at the time. Jeannie and I played with their three girls while Jerry played with their little boy. Their mother taught all five of us girls to bake a cake. It was a white cake with white icing, and we decorated the top with chocolate chips. We had quite a feast devouring the very first cake I ever helped to bake.

Several of our aunts and uncles took us to their homes for a day to visit and play with our cousins. Aunt Barbara treated us to her homemade chili topped with cornbread, and served in her big yellow bowl. She knew it was a special treat for us as well as for her four children, and she made it every visit. When we visited Aunt Ruthie, she usually gave us a little money to spend at the nearby penny candy store. We spent many of those visits eating our candy as Ruthie read stories to us. Aunt Helen let Jeannie and me comb and play with her beautiful, thick, white hair for hours. Rick was the same age as her son, our cousin Jim, and the two of them spent a lot of time together golfing and just being teenagers. Aunt Helen and Uncle Stanley both worked at two different local drive-in theaters. When we were in high school, they each took us to work with them for an evening. We sat in their car and watched the movies while they worked. We always had fun, but those were long evenings because the movies didn't end until well past midnight.

The women in my family always planned a "hen party" while we were visiting so that Jeannie and I could attend. Hen parties were for females only. Each lady brought a covered dish and a dessert to share. The evening was spent eating and visiting. I loved to sit and listen to the adults as they shared thoughts and family history and solved the world's problems. We didn't have the opportunity to listen in on many adult conversations in the Home.

One summer when I was seven or eight years old, Loualtha left us with Joe at a park in Wooster. She returned an hour or so later, and as she got out of the car we saw that she had a strange woman with her. She looked similar to our aunts Beulah and Lenora, but yet she wasn't either one of them. I didn't know who this woman could be. Suddenly, Rick shouted, "Mommy!" and he took off running towards her. I tried to run, too, but tore my new blouse as I jumped off the swing set. I also sustained a small cut on my arm that required a band aid, and I was really more interested in my boo-boo than in this strange lady.

From that point on, during our summer vacations someone in the family brought my mother out of the hospital for a day visit. Her birthday was August 22, so we usually had a family picnic and birthday party sometime around that date for the whole extended family. It was a good opportunity for my mom and for the four of us to see everyone at least once each summer while we were visiting.

My mother definitely remembered Rick. She eventually got to know Jeannie, Jerry, and me. She knew our names and who we were, but I'm not sure she ever completely made the connection that we were her children, because she would sometimes ask me where her babies were. I tried to explain that we were her babies, but that we've grown and are older now. I thought she understood me each time, but then she asked again repeatedly over the years. My mother never completely recovered from her nervous breakdown years before, and was confused about many other things, too. She was obsessed with politics, and most of her stories placed her front and center with some very powerful people. I learned to not attempt to reason with her, but to just agree.

After our vacations we never returned to the Home without new clothes and shoes for school. Loualtha took us shopping at O'Neil's and Marshall's department stores, and we had lunch at a fancy downtown restaurant. She bought each of us a nice shorts-and-top set to wear to any upcoming picnics and to the Medina County Fair. By the end of the day, I usually had at least three new dresses, pajamas, underwear, socks and new shoes.

The trips back to the Home after our vacations were almost unbearable. All four of us were sad to go back. During the return trip, there was so much sniffling and so many tears that Loualtha would stop driving, pull into a rest area, and tell everyone to go ahead and cry. And we cried and cried. Oh, how I wanted to stay with her forever. But that was not possible, and she always made it clear that we would remain at the Home until we had graduated from high school. After our crying subsided, Loualtha would continue the journey to the Home. It was important to finish crying before we got back to the Home, because crying after a vacation was not tolerated. Depending on our supervisor at the time, we were threatened with no more family vacations if there were tears. I've often wondered if it was hard for Loualtha to leave us there each time. Were her trips back home sad for her, or were they a relief for her to be rid of four noisy children?

Loualtha always washed all our clothes before we took them back to the Home, and they smelled fresh and sweet from her laundry detergent. Jeannie told me to keep at least one clothing item tucked away in a drawer, so when I felt sad I could smell that nice laundry smell and feel close to Loualtha.

Some summers Loualtha and Joe broke up our trip back to the Home by driving about halfway to Columbus a few days earlier than we needed to be back at the Home. They booked a room at the Holiday Inn where we could swim, eat out and have fun before being returned. We felt as though we had taken a vacation within our vacation.

We were permitted to have visitors once a month from 1:00–5:00 p.m. on Saturdays and Sundays. Loualtha and Joe tried to visit us at least once a month except during the winter. They usually visited for several hours on

Jeannie, Rick, Jerry and I enjoying a mini
vacation at the Holiday Inn in Columbus.

Aunt Loualtha and Uncle Joe with Janice, Jerry, Jeannie and Rick at a Xenia park during a Saturday afternoon visit.

Saturday afternoons. Sometimes they took us to lunch at a nice restaurant such as the Xenia Hotel or the Golden Lamb in Lebanon. Other times they took us to their motel, where we would have trail bologna, Swiss cheese, crackers and pop, our favorite snack. They tried to vary our activities during these visits. Sometimes we took long car rides, visited all the covered bridges in the area, ate at many different restaurants, or visited their friends in the area. Some visits we went to the movies in downtown Xenia. I remember seeing *Son of Flubber* with Loualtha and Joe on one of their visits. We almost always stopped by the S.S. Kresge Store, where we were each given $1.00 to spend. I could usually find something to buy pretty quickly, but Jerry could never seem to make up his mind, and we all grew impatient with him before he finally spent his dollar.

Loualtha and Joe stayed at the Tecumseh Motel in Xenia during their visits, and eventually became good friends with the owners. By the time I was in high school, Loualtha and Joe had started running the motel during the entire month of November while the owners were away on vacation. It was comforting for me to know they were just down the road. We saw them more often during that month, and were even permitted to go to the motel for Thanksgiving dinner with them. Only seniors were permitted to leave with family for the long Thanksgiving weekend. Loualtha and Joe were not yet running the motel when Rick was a senior, but the rest of us each got a turn staying at the motel with them that weekend.

When I was a senior, I was dating Todd around Thanksgiving. He had graduated that spring and was living and working in Xenia. Unbeknownst to me, he dropped by the motel one evening to introduce himself to Loualtha and Joe and to ask for their permission to take me on a real date over Thanksgiving weekend. They told me that they were impressed with Todd and gave their permission. I spent Thanksgiving weekend with Loualtha and Joe at the motel and, true to their word, they allowed Todd and me to have a real, unchaperoned date. We drove around in his car, went to a rifle range where he taught me to fire his rifle and went out for dinner; just a normal teen date.

School: Academic and Vocational Education

"I forget what I was taught.
I only remember what I have learnt." –Patrick White

Academic Education. All academic classes were housed in the Lincoln Building, a two-story building located directly across the street from the girls' side of the main campus. Kindergarten through 7th grade rooms were located at one end of the building while 8th through 12th grades were at the opposite end. The center of the building housed the administrative offices, school psychologist, guidance counselor, music room, piano practice rooms, and a large library.

While I lived in Peter Pan, each morning, rain or shine, we marched as a group to school with Miss Melvin leading the way. In winter, we were bundled up in coats, scarves, mittens on a shoe string threaded through our coat sleeves so as not to lose them, and boots. Again we marched in two lines, each child holding a partner's hand, with no talking, as Miss Melvin expected us to be quiet as we walked across the campus. We wound our way past the girls' playground to the school building where Miss Melvin watched as we made our way to our classrooms.

We girls wore dresses or blouses and skirts with hems that at least covered our knees. In addition to the state-issued black and white saddle shoes we wore to school, Keds tennis shoes were issued to us for gym class. Those we could keep at the end of the school year. The boys wore blue jeans with t-shirts, button-down shirts or sweaters. Their shoes were brown and also state-issued. When it was rainy or snowy we wore state-issued black rubber boots. They kept our feet dry, but the tops rose higher than my socks and cut into my legs, making them chapped and sore. I think most of us girls hated those boots.

We were Woodrow Wilson High School although the building itself was named the Lincoln Building. Our school day was divided into eight 45-minute periods. We had the same required academic classes as most public schools: Reading, Math, English, Science, Chemistry, Social Studies, Current Events/ Economics, History, Ohio History, and Physical Education. Elective classes were Journalism, Art, Drama and Choir. No foreign language was offered, and that was the only important subject missing from our curriculum. Algebra, geometry and calculus were all rolled into a challenging new program called Set Theory. In English we learned spelling, grammar, writing, punctuation, reading, and some literature. We dissected frogs in Biology. We learned about fossils, leaves, birds, animals and the stars in Science. We performed experiments in Chemistry, trying not to blow up anything. In Current Events we read newspapers and discussed world happenings. We learned about the stock market and pretended to buy our own stocks with $10,000 of play money. We watched with excitement or dismay as our chosen stocks grew...or not.

Students who earned a 3.0 Grade Point Average (GPA) or higher were placed on the Honor Roll. Students with a 3.5 GPA or higher qualified for the Dean's List. Students were given awards such as a pin, a certificate, and a Woodrow Wilson High School pennant. I was on the Honor Roll a few times, but never made the Dean's List. Several of the smartest boys in the Home were in my class, and they were consistently on the Dean's List. Honor Roll students were chosen to escort and greet visitors to the Home as well as to participate in special outings planned just for us. The outing could be anything from dinner at a restaurant to a movie in Dayton, or a Cincinnati Reds game.

Our classes occasionally took field trips to various places around the state. I remember taking several trips to see the State Capitol, the Ohio State Museum, the Air Force Museum at Wright Patterson Air Force Base, Serpent Mound State Park, National Cash Register Corporation (NCR), and the Monsanto Corporation.

Vocational Education was taught at the Barnett Trades Building which was across a side street from the academic building. Ideally, every student attending Woodrow Wilson High School learned a vocational skill, and was sufficiently trained upon graduation to step into a job and start to earn a living. Many times while at the Home I heard the phrase, "No one is going to support you. You must learn to support yourself." I took that advice to heart as I assume most Home kids did.

All students were required to take Typing in 8th and 9th grades. In 9th grade, each girl also spent a semester trying out the two trades that were available to us: Commercial classes (office/administrative) and Cosmetology.

Besides typing, 8th and 9th grade boys tried out the trades that were available to them: Auto Shop, Electric Shop, General/Wood Shop, Hospital Laboratory, Machine Shop, Metal Shop, Print Shop, Farm, and Leather/Shoe Shop. In 10th grade, they picked one as their vocation of choice. Many of the boys' classes produced items or services that were used around the campus.

-   Auto Shop. Repaired employees' cars.
-   Shoe Shop. Resoled our shoes and sold handmade leather items.
-   Metal Shop. Made or repaired many metal items used around campus such as the metal benches, the OSSO Home sign at the main entrance, and the Memorial Day flower baskets.
-   Electric Shop. Fixed electrical appliances and lamps.
-   Print Shop. Printed our monthly news magazine, *The Home Review*, written by Journalism Class students.

Several girls who were interested in becoming Dental Assistants were assigned to the dental office in order to learn that vocation. A few boys trained

My senior chemistry class with Mrs. Lane on a field trip to Monsanto Labs.
I was the only girl in this class, and Mrs. Lane allowed my dear friend
Phyllis, far left, to accompany me.

as technicians in the Hospital lab where they were taught to analyze urine tests and blood counts as part of their training.

I wanted to be a nurse, and discussed with our vocational principal the possibility of helping out at the hospital by shadowing the nurses, learning to take temperatures, making beds, and providing comfort to the patients. He wouldn't allow it; although, within just a few years after I graduated a similar program was initiated. I like to think that I planted that idea and smoothed the way for other girls to be able to learn this vocation.

All girls in 8th and 9th grades were required to take Home Economics, spending one semester in Cooking and another semester in Sewing. In 8th grade sewing class we spent a good deal of time learning to hand sew and baste before we could move on to a real sewing project. We learned to sew on old treadle sewing machines. These machines seemed to me to be much easier to control than today's electric machines, but they lacked all the fancy bells and whistles. Our first project was to make a white apron with colored binding to wear in cooking class. In 9th grade we made pajamas (pink and pretty, much more appealing than the ugly hospital pajamas!) and our choice of another item of clothing. I made a blue corduroy jumper. By the time I left the Home, I felt as though I could sew just about anything.

I loved cooking classes. We not only learned to cook, but we also learned how to correctly organize and clean the kitchen, and set the table. We ate everything we cooked, and learned to use proper table manners. We started by making simple breakfast foods such as baked apples, hot cereal, and cinnamon coffee cake. We then moved on to a very simple chili con carne recipe that I still sometimes make today. We finally learned to cook complete dinners such as pork chops, mashed potatoes, and creamed peas. I believe, though, that we actually spent the most time learning to bake—cookies, cakes, pies, and even a fancy chocolate torte. We made plain vanilla cream pies from scratch until we could almost make them in our sleep. Rick used to say, "They don't let orphan girls leave the Home until they can bake a pie!"

The Auto Shop was located directly beneath our cooking lab. A few times we sneaked and threw cookies out the window to the boys below. Both Rick and Jerry took Auto Shop as their chosen trade, but neither one stayed in this field after he graduated. I'm not sure if any of my cookies ever really reached them, but I certainly tried.

All students were required to choose a vocation in the 10th grade. I chose Commercial class where I learned typing, shorthand, filing, bookkeeping, business math and business machines. Those girls who didn't choose Commercial classes went into Cosmetology. The junior and senior Cosmetology students provided free salon services to students, and charged a nominal fee to employees. By the time graduation rolled around, they had already taken their State Board exams, and were eligible to receive their license to practice.

My Commercial classes were easy for me, and I earned good grades. By the end of 12th grade I was ready to enter the workforce with a typing speed of 80+ words per minute and a shorthand speed of 140 words per minute. I had earned all of the filing certificates available. Before graduation, our teachers, Mrs. Harner and Mr. Stein, drove the seniors in my class to Dayton to take the Federal Civil Service exams. Mrs. Harner stressed to us that we were as prepared to work in an office as students graduating from any business college. I know she was correct because I later worked with girls who graduated from these schools, who had far fewer skills than we Home girls had acquired.

I worked really hard in my Commercial classes, but I always felt as though there was a little asterisk beside my name, a reminder that none of this really mattered for me, that I would never use any of this office stuff, because I would be a nurse.

We enjoyed a well-stocked library at the Home. I don't know how many books it contained, but I was always able to find an interesting book to read. In elementary and junior high grades, we spent class time each week at the library. In the younger grades, the librarian read stories to us. As we got older and could read, we learned how to find our own books to check out. We were taught the Dewey Decimal System so that we could find books but also help the librarian put them back on the shelves. The library contained encyclopedias and reference materials to use for homework assignments, reports, and term papers. My favorite book in junior high was *The Autobiography of Louisa May Alcott*.

When I was in 6th or 7th grade, many of the older girls were reading a new book, *The Carpetbaggers* by Harold Robbins. It contained a really steamy love scene—steamy at least by 1963 standards. I wanted to check out this book to see what all the fuss was about, but it seemed to always be out in circulation. That is, until one day, there it was, right on the shelf where it belonged. I grabbed that book and boldly walked up to the desk to check it out.

The librarian, who just a year or two earlier had been my 5th grade teacher, took one look at the title of my book and said, "Janice, you can't take this book."

"Why not?" I asked.

And that's when her face turned a brighter red than any face I had ever seen before. "There are things in this book you shouldn't know about."

I didn't want to embarrass her further, so I didn't say anything more. I was pretty embarrassed myself, but now my curiosity was piqued more than ever before. I really wanted to read that book. But, alas, I had to wait until 9th grade when I checked it out of the library without any problem at all. After all that, I can't even remember the much anticipated steamy love scene.

We met for Phys Ed twice a week; once for gym, and once for swimming. We started gym class each week by changing into our gym suits—a blue one-piece outfit with snaps up the front, a belted waist and short bottoms. We then lined up in a straight line, held our hands out with palms down as our teacher, Miss Whilding, made her way across the line of girls and clipped our fingernails. No excuses, no matter our age, our nails were gone. Now class could begin.

Our gym classes taught basketball, volleyball, dodge ball, softball, trampoline, running, tumbling, and calisthenics. My favorites were trampoline and basketball. We had a large trampoline, and two girls could jump at a time while all the other girls circled the trampoline to watch and provide a safety net. We did somersaults and flips, always assured that we would be shoved back onto the trampoline by our friends, if necessary. We occasion-

"There are things in this book you shouldn't know about."

ally had student teachers in Phys Ed. They seemed to all enjoy calisthenics—stretching, push-ups, running, and jumping jacks—more than our usual games.

Miss Whilding ruled not only in the gym, but also on the playground and at camp. She definitely had her favorites, girls who were for the most part more athletic than I was, but I managed to stay in her good graces most of the time. Any misstep was often her cue to remark, "What do you think this is, your birthday?" Funny, but to my knowledge, she never said those words to anyone on her actual birthday.

We were so lucky to be one of the only schools in Ohio to have an indoor swimming pool. Back then this was almost unheard of. Swimming was a required weekly graded class for grades 1 through 11, so only kindergarteners and seniors didn't take swimming classes. We wore ill-fitting cotton tank suits. These red suits offered no modesty whatsoever, and when wet, barely stayed on.

We started our swimming lessons with the crawl, backstroke and treading water, before moving on to swimming under water, surface diving, underwater strokes, and cannonballs. Before long we were having fun in swim class. We swam laps and races, played water dodge ball, dove for items at the bottom of the pool, and perfected cannonballs and somersaults from the side of the pool into the water. We learned to dive from the diving board—forward dives, backward dives, forward and backward flips. We learned to dive and then stay underwater the entire length of the pool until we came up for air in the shallow end. Most of us became very good swimmers.

Some of the visiting basketball team members told us they enjoyed playing against us because after the games, win or lose, they could take a dip in our pool. It was truly a novelty, and a blessing for us Home kids.

I took art only when it was a required class before 9th grade. My first teacher, Ms. Madge McCoy, was most interested in clay and ceramics. She used her kiln to fire our creations that we had painted and glazed. We were taught to draw and finger paint. She was replaced by Mr. John Norris, who threw out the kiln and concentrated on his passion, painting and drawing. He inspired his students to enter their drawings and posters in district contests for awards in areas such as safety and conservation. Ms. Rebecca Carter then replaced Mr. Norris. She taught us new techniques like papier-mâché, silk screen, rug making, stitchery, mosaics, and linoleum blocks for Christmas cards. We made potholders on a little loom, and learned to crochet just enough to finish off the edges. I enjoyed that little bit of crocheting enough to inspire me to master this craft, and it became a lifelong passion for me.

When choosing elective classes in high school, I decided I enjoyed choir and drama better than art. I chose two years in each of those classes. I'm glad I made those choices because I have great memories of sitting next to Jeannie in the alto section of the choir. In drama class, I learned to work through some of my shyness and fear of public speaking. I made good friends in both classes.

My Teachers

"In recalling their school years, students mostly remember their teachers, and not the courses they took." –Unknown

The teachers in our school at the Home were dedicated. They not only taught classes, but frequently volunteered with other activities such as sports, scouting and other after-school clubs, music programs, and dances, to help make our time in the Home more well-rounded and fun. I loved inviting my teachers to join my cottage for lunch or dinner, and most happily accepted.

Our dedicated teachers helped to provide an excellent education f(
of us. Out of the 37 students in my high school graduation class, we proudly
produced a clinical psychologist, a city planner, a mortician, a hotel owner, a
hospital IT specialist, a manager at HUD, a social worker, a magazine co-own-
er, an Army officer, an executive assistant at a large university, a physician, a
college professor, two machinists who remained with the same employer their
entire careers, two engineers, and me.

I want to mention some of these teachers who made an especially positive
impression on me.

Miss Augusta Stanfield, Kindergarten.

I began kindergarten about three weeks after arriving at the Home. All
children were required to attend school during the day, and although Jerry
was only four years old at the time, he was placed in kindergarten with me.
This became my favorite time of the day because I could be with Jerry and
have fun learning new stories and songs. I will always remember Miss Stanfield for her kindness in allowing Jerry and me to sit together, although she
often scolded us for talking too much.

Kindergarten students attended only in the mornings, and about halfway
through the morning we took a rest break. We were given a little braided rug to
lie on. Of course I didn't go to sleep, but found a way to amuse myself. I tied
the stringy ends of my rug to the rug of the person beside me. And I got caught.

"Janice, what are you doing?" Miss Stanfield scolded. "Now you untie
those rugs."

So I started trying to untie them. So many strings, such a tangled mess. I
started using my teeth to untangle the strings. That made it even worse.

I learned a lesson that I carry with me today, "Janice, don't ever get a knot
wet. That only makes it harder to untangle."

I couldn't get the knot out, and rest period was over. I'm not sure what
happened with those rugs, but Miss Stanfield most likely had to cut out the
knot. And I never did that again!

Mrs. Lenora Mart, First Grade.

Mrs. Mart was a middle-aged woman with beautiful short white hair. She
was a bright spot during my days living in Pan 6. No matter how bad things

got in my cottage, she seemed to make everything better. She gave wonderful hugs that made me feel warm, safe and loved. She very encouragingly taught us to read, write and do simple arithmetic.

Our class was performing in a play with all the other primary grades. As part of my role I needed to skip, but didn't know how. Mrs. Mart and Miss Stanfield kindly spent part of their lunch hour in the days shortly before the play to give me skipping lessons. We three skipped around the kindergarten room, over and over until I had finally mastered this skill.

One day I wrote a little story about playing in the snow. Mrs. Mart was as proud and excited as a parent might be. She encouraged me to read my story to the staff in the principal's office as well as in a couple of the older classrooms. I wish I still had a copy of that little story.

Mrs. Mart took our class for a field trip to her dairy farm. We met her husband, Harold, who grew fruits and vegetables. We learned to make home-made ice cream, and added farm-grown strawberries. It was a great field trip.

Mrs. Betsey Peterson, Third Grade.

Mrs. Peterson was full of energy. I think I learned as much about life from her as I did school lessons. One day Suzanne, one of the taller girls in the class, came to school in the ugliest dress I had ever seen, one that she had obviously outgrown. One of the seamstresses in the Home's tailor shop had sewn a nine-inch wide piece of fabric to the bottom of her dress that clashed with the rest of the fabric. Mrs. Peterson had to have noticed how hideous the dress looked.

"Suzanne, that is the prettiest dress I've ever seen, Mrs. Peterson kindly exclaimed. "Come up to front of the room so everyone can see it."

With obvious reluctance, Suzanne shuffled to the front of the room. "Now twirl around like a princess showing off her beautiful gown." As Suzanne turned around, Mrs. Peterson pulled out her own chair into the center of the room. "I don't think the students in the back of the room can see you, Suzanne. Stand up in this chair so everyone can see your beautiful dress."

I'm pretty sure Suzanne was dying inside with embarrassment; I was embarrassed for her.

On another occasion, Mrs. Peterson came to school one day wearing the same dress that she had worn the previous day. Of course, we ever observant third graders immediately noticed and called out her transgression. A sad expression crossed Mrs. Peterson's face as she acknowledged that, yes, this was the same dress. She then explained that her dear friend's husband had died the day before, and she went directly to her friend without first going home after school. She stayed with her all night and then returned to school that morning. She followed the explanation with an apology for wearing the same dress. After hearing her explanation, I was ashamed of myself and my classmates. We had intruded into Mrs. Peterson's personal life and rendered an unfair judgment. I promised myself that I would never again comment on someone wearing the same clothes two days in a row, because they also may have a personal reason for doing so.

These two memories have stayed with me throughout my life. I can still feel Mrs. Peterson's kindness and compassion to both Suzanne and her dear friend. No one dared to criticize or make fun of Suzanne's dress after Mrs. Peterson's kind compliments. What a wise way to turn an ugly dress into a beautiful gown. Mrs. Peterson taught me that it's important to be there for friends no matter the personal inconvenience. I also learned not to hastily judge someone's clothing or appearance.

Mr. Paul Boykin, Seventh Grade.

A young black man, Mr. Boykin was my first male teacher. He was an ex-pupil who had also grown up in the Home. He came from a large family and was a star athlete while in the Home, as were his brothers.

I liked Mr. Boykin's class. He made school fun while he taught us responsibility and the importance of studying. We started each morning by reciting the Pledge of Allegiance to the flag. Then we were obliged to state a famous quotation and its author from memory, starting each day from a different location in the room and without repeating what had been stated previously.

For instance, "Ask not what your country can do for you, ask what you can do for your country." —John F. Kennedy

The penalty for not being ready with an unused quotation was one whack with Mr. Boykin's paddle in front of the class. I learned to be prepared with a totally new quotation or two as a back-up in case my chosen one had already been stated before my turn.

Postal zip codes came into being while I was in Mr. Boykin's class. He made it easier to remember the zip code for Xenia (45385). He explained that he always wanted to get all As which would give him a 4.0 average, he graduated and left the Home in '53, and he hoped to live to be 85 years old. So, 45385, who could ever forget that?

Correct spelling was of utmost importance to Mr. Boykin. He provided a weekly spelling list to study, with a test at the end of the week. He would pronounce each word and then use it in a sentence as we wrote down the word on our paper. My favorite humorous example is this one: "Influence. I opened the window and in-flew-ence." The penalty for a misspelled word was again a whack with Mr. Boykin's paddle at the front of the room. I don't remember what word I misspelled that year, but I remember both the pain and embarrassment I felt. The experience motivated me to study harder so I would never feel that paddle again.

Shortly after lunch break on November 22, 1963, Mr. Boykin pulled his stool to the front of the room. "President Kennedy has just been assassinated," he sadly told us, tears running down his cheeks.

I knew this was important, and I knew something really bad had happened to our president, but I had no idea what assassinated meant.

"What does assassinated mean?" I tapped Dennis, who was sitting in front of me, on the shoulder.

He quickly replied, "He got shot, stupid!"

I looked outside at the flag not yet lowered to half-mast, feeling that the world would never be the same. For the next three days the world seemed to stop as we gathered around the television to watch the solemn funeral ceremonies. I cried as little John-John saluted his daddy's casket as it passed by; such sadness on his third birthday.

Mrs. Helen Cotner, Journalism.

My favorite teacher of all was Mrs. Cotner, my Journalism teacher all four years of high school. We wrote news articles for *The Home Review* in her class.

Mrs. Cotner was my 9th grade English teacher, and she placed a great deal of emphasis on teaching us to write. Each week she would walk around the class with a shoe box filled with pictures. She held the box up high as we each reached in and took out a picture without looking at the other pictures first. We would then write a couple of paragraphs about the picture. Mrs. Cotner marked up our papers with her red pencil. She hated for us to use the word 'very.' She explained that we should have the vocabulary to use the right word instead of being lazy and using 'very.' For example, very hot should be replaced with torrid, burning, boiling or some other word. Very tall should be gigantic or something similar. With this memory, I need to be sure I haven't used the word 'very' too many places here in my story.

By my senior year, Mrs. Cotner treated me as though I were a grownup, a friend. She later told me she did not come to my graduation because she didn't want to break down saying goodbye to me. We stayed in touch for several years after I left the Home; she wrote to me through the illness and death of her husband, Bob. I still miss her.

Mr. Jack Newhouse, Science and Photo Club.

I fondly remember Mr. Newhouse because he taught me two valuable life lessons. A skeleton, Lilly, stood in a corner of his science room. Mr. Newhouse told us that Lilly was a smoker. He talked about the dangers of smoking during a time when most people smoked. I have never smoked, and I give Mr. Newhouse some of the credit for that decision. Mr. Newhouse also reminded us often about the importance of brushing our teeth properly and regularly. He emphasized that we should always brush up and down so we don't end up with grooves in our teeth. I still occasionally think of him as I'm brushing my teeth...up and down, of course.

Mr. Michael Berry, English Literature.

I was in Mr. Berry's class his first year of teaching at the Home. He was young and full of new ideas for teaching English. He had a habit of constantly saying the word "see" when he spoke in class. One day, we all decided before class that we would count how many times he said "see" that day. As the class progressed, and the count went higher, we started giggling. Poor Mr. Berry had no idea what we were doing, but he joined in the laughter. I don't remember the final count, but he did break 100 "sees" that day. This was such a mean trick to play on him, but it was such a fun and memorable day for us.

On Fridays we watched movies in his class, mostly documentaries about the Air Force. I remember one in particular about big silos opening up from the ground as part of our missile defense program from the '60s. It made me feel secure knowing our Air Force was ready and able to defend our country.

I remember Mr. Berry with guilt, too, because I took advantage of him by cheating in his class...the only time I cheated in school. I enjoyed his classes until he gave the assignment to memorize the "Prologue to the Canterbury Tales" in Old English. I took shorthand classes at the time and had become quite proficient. I wrote out the entire Prologue in shorthand and labeled the paper, "Biology Notes" printed in regular English. With my seat next to the window sill, it was easy to place my notes there and transcribe them. I made an A, but I know I deserved an F.

Mrs. Louise Harner, Commercial.

Mrs. Harner was my shorthand, typing, filing and business teacher for three years. Her skills were top notch. In teaching shorthand, she could dictate letters and articles at proper speeds. She started at 60 words per minute (wpm) and then she gradually increased her dictation speed to 80, 100, 120, 140, 160 and 180 wpm at a rate dependent on the skill of the students. To pass from one level to the next, we were required to transcribe a five-minute dictation with 95 percent accuracy. When I graduated, I had passed 120 wpm and had come close to passing the 140 wpm level, having achieved only 94 percent accuracy. One student in the class routinely practiced at 180 wpm because she was preparing for her 160 wpm test, and we all practiced with her to improve our speeds.

Mrs. Harner was a stickler for accuracy. She expected our typing assignments to be completely error free before they were turned in. We typed on manual, and later electric typewriters. An error meant starting over and over again until the assignment was perfect. Fifty years later, I still aim for perfection, but am thankful that computers allow us to make corrections without tearing up the page and starting over...and over...and over.

Mr. Charles Minch, History, Economics, Senior Problems, and Local and Current Events.

Mr. Minch was both my History teacher and later my Current Events teacher. One thing that has stuck in my memory about him is that he never seemed to smile.

Each student was given a weekly news magazine to study. We took turns giving our classmates a weekly test from this magazine. Several members of my class hounded the test giver each week to hand out the answers to the test before class. I remember my distress when this group approached me and wanted my answers. I didn't want to cheat. I remember being torn, and the discomfort of peer pressure. I'm not sure how I avoided giving the answers away.

Mr. Minch had a passion for teaching about the Civil War, and I developed an interest in it, but it never became my passion. Jerry loved Mr. Minch's class, and became even more enthusiastic about the Civil War than Mr. Minch. Jerry read about it incessantly, and could answer just about any Civil War question thrown at him. He knew every battle and every battlefield. Several years ago when I lived near Manassas, Virginia, Jerry spent several days walking the Manassas Battlefield until he had familiarized himself with the entire site. I credit Mr. Minch for awakening that passion in him.

During our Current Events class in 1968, we conducted a mock presidential election. Grades 9-12 were eligible to vote. The candidates were Hubert Humphrey, who won 55% of the votes, Richard Nixon, who won 36% of the votes, and George Wallace, who won 9% of the votes. I voted for Richard Nixon in our little election.

Mr. Glendon Lakes, Drivers Ed and Wood Shop.

An ex-pupil of the Home, Mr. Lakes was our Drivers Ed teacher. He taught us to drive during the summer before our senior year. We drove only on the Home grounds, so no temporary license was required. Many of us had never been behind the wheel of a car before. We learned on a standard transmission car. Luckily Mr. Lakes had a clutch and brake, too, on his side of the car. We were put into groups of four—a driver and three backseat observers. I was not a natural when it came to learning how to use the clutch. The boys in the backseat thought it was funny as I struggled to put the car in gear to drive uphill. As the gears ground louder and louder, Mr. Lakes would laugh and say, "Grind me out a pound." My favorite quote from Mr. Lakes was, "Manhandle that car, woman!"

Mr. Lakes taught a Saturday morning class for senior girls. We learned to change a light bulb, wire a lamp, replace the inside of a toilet tank, change a tire—things that would help us become more independent after we left the

Home. The boys took a different class on Saturday mornings with Sgt. Gaither, the dietitian. He taught them to cook simple menus to sustain themselves.

Mr. John Norris, Art.

Mr. Norris was another ex-pupil of the Home. An extremely talented artist, he painted the pictures of Snow White and the Seven Dwarfs that adorned the hospital room where we spent our first two weeks at the Home in isolation. Mr. Norris was also a semi-professional hockey player with the Dayton Gems. He often provided tickets free of charge for us Home kids to attend his games. That was a generous treat, and it was fun to watch him play.

Musical Programs

"Music education should not be a privilege for a lucky few, it should be a part of every child's world of possibility." –Hillary Clinton

Lunchtime was a flurry of activity for students who chose to play musical instruments. We Home students were fortunate that we were able to learn to play just about any instrument we wanted. All fourth graders took flutophone lessons and learned about different instruments. In fifth grade students could choose an instrument they wanted to learn, and begin taking lessons.

I chose to play the piano. My first piano teacher was Mr. Cochran, who also taught stringed instruments. He was replaced by Mr. Stanley Gunn, who taught piano in addition to his duties as Choir Director and Church Organist. I loved to watch Mr. Gunn play piano. He seemed to be able to play any musical piece.

There were fifteen–twenty piano students each year. Our weekly, one-on-one piano lessons were integrated into our school day as a graded class. Practice was scheduled every school day following lunch. Five or six piano rooms located near the music room were filled with students practicing their lessons. A couple of the rooms even had two pianos so we could practice duets with other students. Practice was fun for me, and I learned a lot from the other students.

During my junior year I switched from piano to organ. My organ practices and lessons with Mr. Gunn were now in the Chapel. The Chapel was somewhat isolated, the first building near the Home entrance. I was given a key so that I could practice on my own each day. I could never figure out how to lock the Chapel door from the inside to be sure no one wandered in while I was practicing. This made me feel a bit insecure. I took organ lessons for only that one year. I didn't like practicing alone in the Chapel, and I didn't enjoy playing the organ so much as I had playing the piano.

Our annual piano recital was held each spring. We were able to invite guests to watch us perform, so I usually invited my brothers, sister, and my boyfriend. For my last recital piece I played *Fur Elise* by Beethoven. I also played a duet with another girl, *The Parade of the Tin Soldiers* by Leon Jessel. There was no recital for organists but I did occasionally play for Communion services at the Chapel.

I wanted to be a great pianist, but I could never just sit down and sight read a piece. I needed a lot of practice before I could really play a song. I've always been a little disappointed in myself that I never learned to play as well as I had envisioned myself playing. But I still enjoy playing my piano, and mostly stick with easy hymns or children's songs.

Lunchtime was also a busy time for the orchestra students. This talented group of musicians performed at concerts, plays, and special events throughout the year as well as at the graduation Commencement service. Jeannie played violin and was a member of the orchestra.

Rick and Jerry were in band. Mr. Schumacher, the director, taught them both to play the trumpet. I thought he was a musical genius, as he taught every band member to play his chosen instrument. Sometimes his lessons were one-on-one, and other times he taught in small groups. The band room was in the school building, and students had lessons scheduled throughout the school day. Band students advanced from beginner's band through Elementary, Intermediate and finally concert band. A smaller group was chosen to play in dance band. While both boys and girls played in these bands, only boys were members of the marching band. It was considered one of the military companies, and not available to girls. This band participated in the Sunday Retreat Parades, Memorial Day Parade, and 40 et 8 Field Day activities. It was organized the same as the two battalion companies, with a band major and similar officers.

Boys who played the trumpet were called upon to play *Taps* at both the Memorial Day and Veterans' Day Programs. Rick and Jerry were both chosen to play *Taps* during their final high school years.

Girls were part of the Concert Band that treated the rest of us to several concerts throughout the year. We had our own band shell at the Home, and when the weather was amenable the concerts were held there. Winter and Christmas concerts were held in the Auditorium.

In the summer the band presented concerts and marched in parades all around Ohio for conventions of veterans' organizations, civic groups, and festivals. They rarely returned home without a trophy or medal. Mr. Schumacher was often invited to address these host organizations to familiarize them with the Home and its facilities, activities, and purpose. These host organizations often gifted the Home with band instruments or money. The students could claim their band instruments only until they graduated or left the Home, at which time they were returned to the band director to be used by other students.

Vocal music was a part of our school curriculum, with Mr. Gunn teaching music classes to kindergarten through 8th grade students, as well as directing the Home's high school choir. I took choir in 9th and 10th grades, with practice held during school hours. The choir performed each week during Chapel services.

I felt fortunate to be in choir the year Mr. Gunn directed a musical performance of Cinderella. I was part of the chorus and also danced the waltz at the Prince's Ball. I wish I could remember who played the roles of Cinderella and Prince Charming. I still sing three of those songs as part of my grandchildren's lullaby routine: *Now You Are Fair Cinderella*, *The Clock Is Queer*, and *Sister, Sister Come Aside and Speak to Me*.

Drama Class and Performances

"I love acting. It is so much more real than life." –Oscar Wilde

Our drama class, taught by Mr. J. R. Rooney, was one of the most dynamic and energetic groups on campus. I took drama as an elective class in both 11th and 12th grades. Stagecraft was also incorporated into this class. I found that designing, constructing, painting and setting up scenery were almost as enjoyable as acting. I loved acting until the actual day of the performance, when the thought always popped into my head, "Why did I ever sign up for this?" At that point I wanted to run, but I managed to get through it every time.

Mr. Rooney's drama classes presented at least one play a year, and sometimes as many as three in a school year. Under his scriptwriter name, Wayne Lindsay, Mr. Rooney wrote several of the plays that were performed by his classes.

Performance night was a big deal on campus. Everyone attended—children, supervisors, teachers, employees, ex-pupils, representatives from veterans' organizations, and local residents. The Print Shop students made programs to hand out to guests. The Home Advisory Committee provided ushers.

During my senior year, Gary Price and I had lead roles as siblings Kate and Jake Chalice in a Wayne Lindsay production, *The Kiss of Death*. Jake Chalice was the new owner of the Chalice Mansion. The previous owner had hidden gold in the tower, and his beautiful granddaughter was determined to sneak past the new owner to claim the gold for herself. The production was complete with spider webs, bats, vampires, thunder and lightning, as well as memorable characters such as escapees from a mental institution, strange servants, misplaced neighbors, a sheriff, a coroner, and a villain.

My favorite line in this play was, "'Won't you come into my parlor?' said the spider to the fly," recited to Gary in an effort to get him to follow me into the spooky tower.

In third grade I was the lead snowflake in a play called *In Santa's Workshop*. I still remember my line, "We must go, too, or we will melt." Jerry was also a snowflake who stood right beside me. I remember that line so well today because Jerry remembered it too; he made it his little goodbye quip, and repeated it to me often over the years.

When I was in second or third grade, I was a flower in a children's play entitled, *The Land of Dreams Come True*. The elementary and intermediate classes also performed several other plays while I was in grade school: *The Long Road to Bethlehem*, *The Gifts of the Children*, *The Christmas Eve Visitor*, and *The Magi's Gift*.

One summer while I was in junior high Mr. Rooney led a summer acting program. We performed Mark Twain's *The Adventures of Huckleberry Finn*. My role was playing Aunt Polly. I had so much fun that summer, and it whetted my appetite enough that I joined the drama class in high school.

While many plays were performed during my time at the Home, there are some I recall. Rick was also in drama and he performed in several of these. The following are the plays that were written by Wayne Lindsay which was the pen name for Mr. Rooney

Armistice (Revised by Wayne Lindsay)
Bolt from the Blue
Death by the Numbers
Flashback
The Ark
The Gang's All Here (performed by Rick's 1965 Senior Class)

Other Plays I Remember:
A Mid-Summer Night's Dream
Arsenic and Old Lace
Best Foot Forward
Comedy of Errors
I Remember Mama
Ladies in Retirement
My Sister Eileen
Stalag 17
The Man Who Came to Dinner
You Can't Take it With You

A Fun Drama Memory

During my junior year in drama, I was cast as an older woman in one of our performances. It was dress rehearsal evening and Irene, a senior Cosmetology student, was our hair stylist. Irene fixed my hair, and when she was finished, she grabbed the silver hairspray and colored my hair. My hair had a beautiful, shiny glow, and as it dried it became very stiff. Mr. Rooney took one look at it and rushed me straight backstage to Irene.

"Irene, which can of hairspray did you use on Janice?"

Irene looked at my hair as a look of horror flashed across her face. She realized what had happened.

Irene grabbed the can and sheepishly replied, "Silver Enamel."

Everyone began to laugh, especially Mr. Rooney, who thought it was hysterically funny to "knock" on my hair, which by now was almost as hard as a rock. I don't remember if I laughed or cried. My hair stayed in place overnight, all of the following day and throughout the final performance that evening.

The following day Mr. Rooney walked into English class carrying a huge can of turpentine. He walked over to my desk in the front row, and slammed that big can down. Then he started laughing and laughing. He laughed until he cried, and then he laughed some more. The whole class was laughing and I could only laugh too, as he "knocked" on my hair one last time.

Extracurricular Activities

"Guard well your spare moments. They are like uncut diamonds. Discard them and their value will never be known. Improve them and they will become the brightest gems in a useful life." –Ralph Waldo Emerson

The Association of Ex-Pupils (AXP) owned and renovated the old library building for students to use for clubs and hobbies. Their vision was to create a space for children to meet to build models, collect stamps and coins, knit and crochet, do needle craft, leather craft, weaving, ceramics, and pottery. I don't know if the building ever housed all of these crafts, but I remember that both the Model Club and Photo Club met there. This building today is the location of our AXP Museum.

I joined the Photo Club during my junior year. Our leader was Mr. Newhouse, the science and biology teacher. While he developed most of the film, we were able to go in the darkroom and observe. We learned to make black and white copies of just about any picture we wanted. We learned to take portraits of ourselves and friends. I spent most of my time learning to tint black and white pictures to make them appear as color pictures.

I had my senior picture taken professionally at a studio in Xenia with the rest of my class, but ordered only one 8"x 10" color photo. I took that picture to Photo Club and made many black and white copies in several different sizes to hand out to my friends and family. This was a considerable cost savings for me. The Photo Club also offered this service to other seniors. I don't know who paid for all of our supplies—equipment, paper, developing fluids—quite an expense.

4-H Clubs were popular at the Home. The Cadet Rangers raised dairy calves, sheep and rabbits at the farm. Jerry was in the rabbit club for most of his high school years. I joined the Cadet Stitchers for a year or two. We made clothing to enter in the Greene County Fair for judging. I didn't personally win any ribbons, but some of the girls were quite talented and won ribbons each year.

I joined Girl Scouts in junior high as a Cadette Scout. Mrs. Mary Lane, our math and chemistry teacher, was the Girl Scout leader at the Home for many years. Her daughter Susan helped out with our troop. She was in her 20s, and taught us girls how to fix our hair and apply makeup, as well as helped us to master our scouting skills. My supervisor, Mrs. Purtell, was close friends with Mrs. Lane, and she joined us in some of our scouting activities.

In Photo Club, I used this senior picture, taken professionally in Xenia, to make pictures to give to family and friends.

The summer between 7th and 8th grades three other Home girls and I attended a two-week scout camp held at Camp Whip Poor Will near Morrow, Ohio. We each received a $40 Campership award from the Girl Scout Council in order to attend.

We sold Girl Scout Cookies around campus to help support our projects. We sold our cookies to both students and employees. Back then, the cookies were a mere 50 cents a box!

I stayed in Scouts only until I had completed the Cadette level. I enjoyed being in Scouts, but some of the older girls told me that the more popular girls don't join Scouts. Wanting to be liked as I entered high school, I dropped out. I think that as a result I missed out on making some nice friends and experiencing a host of interesting and valuable opportunities.

Sports

"Team rah, team rah! Rah, rah, team!
Who? Team! Who? Team!
Who? Team, team, team!" –A Favorite Home Cheer

Who doesn't remember that cheer? We were the Woodrow Wilson High School Cadets. There weren't too many opportunities for girls to participate in sports. Some of the girls did join the Girls Athletic Association (GAA) and played intramural basketball and volleyball against other high school teams in the area. While I was never interested in participating in sports, I was a great spectator.

Cheerleading was a popular activity for girls. The cheerleaders helped to provide both spirit and enthusiasm for the football and basketball teams. The girls who wanted to try out for cheerleading spent many summer evenings on the playground practicing. Sometimes it seemed that most of the girls were practicing and cheering right along with them. It was great fun and we all knew the cheers. Although I tried out once or twice, I never made the cheering squad. Jeannie was a cheerleader for all four years of high school, and she was really good at it.

The Home offered a variety of sports for boys: football, basketball, baseball, wrestling, track and field, cross country and rifle team. We were in the Mid-Miami League most of the time I was in the Home. We joined the Dayton Suburban League during my last year of high school. Our Coach, Mousie Eisenhower, was legendary. He took many teams to state meets while coaching at the Home. He was unique in that he coached three major sports: football, basketball, and track and field. He was coaching at the Home long before I arrived, and was still there for several years after I left.

We played numerous schools during my years in the Home. Some that stand out in my memory are Spring Valley, Bellbrook, Yellow Springs, Lebanon, Lemon-Monroe, Fairborn, Miamisburg, and Cedarville. I know there were many more schools that I've forgotten over the years.

All the high school boys were required to participate in football, with the exception of those on the cross country team. Because our school population was small, we needed every single boy in order to be able to field a team. Over the years, the Home had some extremely good teams, and even won a few state championships.

Our football field didn't have lights until my last year in the Home, so we played our home games on Saturday afternoons. Our band couldn't play at half-time because all the band boys were on the football team. If only girls had been permitted to join the marching band! I enjoyed watching the visiting bands provide the half-time shows. The Junior Class operated the concession stand at the games as part of its fundraising program. I had fun going to the games and cheering along with the crowd.

In 1968–69, the AXP undertook a huge fundraising project to update our Brewster Football Field. They raised enough money to add lights, a new scoreboard and a concession stand that also housed dressing rooms with showers and bathrooms. That was the year we joined the Dayton Suburban League, and we were now able to host evening games.

Basketball was my favorite sport, and I didn't miss many games during my high school years. I sat in the bleachers with my girlfriends. Jerry never played basketball so he usually sat nearby, and we all cheered our hearts out for our Cadets. When I had a boyfriend on the team, it made the game even more exciting. And when he waved or sneaked a wink while playing, it was the best feeling in the world.

We had some excellent basketball teams over the years. I believe it was the 1965–66 team that had gone far in the post-season tournament. I cried along with many of the other girls as we finally went down in defeat in a close, exciting game. With that game, my love for basketball was born, and I still enjoy watching it today.

One of my favorite competing high schools was the Ohio School for the Deaf. This team traveled to the Home from Columbus every year. They were quiet, but always presented a challenge. It was interesting to watch as they used sign language to communicate with each other and the coach.

The Indiana Soldiers' and Sailors' Children's Home, located in Knightstown, Indiana, was our sister school and sister Home. The Indiana Home was founded in 1865 to provide care, education and maintenance for the orphaned and destitute children of Civil War Union Army veterans. It closed in 2009. We played basketball against their team each year, rotating between the two locations. Seniors, basketball team members, and cheerleaders from the visiting location were invited guests of the other school for the weekend.

When I was a junior, students from the Indiana Home visited our Home. As an honor roll student that semester, I was chosen to be my cottage's hostess for one of our visitors. I gave this Indiana senior a tour of our campus, shared my room with her, and accompanied her to meals, the basketball game, and a Saturday night dance after the game. Two disc jockeys from my favorite radio station, WING, Steve Kirk and Jay Elliott, provided music for the evening. I still have Steve's autograph from that evening. My Indiana visitor and I wrote letters back and forth for a short time until she graduated and left her Home.

My senior year we traveled to the Indiana Home for the weekend. I decided I liked our Home much better than that Home. Their grounds were smaller than ours, and not so beautiful. The Indiana girls all stayed in dormitories rather than two-person rooms like ours. During my visit I slept on a top bunk bed in a large dormitory with about twenty girls. The meals at the Indiana Home were served cafeteria style rather than family style, something different and fun for us. Their food was just as good as ours. We made new friends, enjoyed the basketball game and the dance, and our team wrapped up the weekend with a victory!

Baseball, wrestling and cross-country were not spectator sports for girls, and I don't know why we were prevented from attending any of those meets. Jerry was a wrestler, and I would have loved to watch him compete.

Rick was a pole vaulter, and I did attend some of his meets. There were track meets, both home and away, some weekends when Loualtha and Joe visited, and they took us to watch Rick compete at nearby high schools. Rick was pretty good, and placed in many of his meets. I was proud of my big brother, and I felt so special when he let me get my picture taken holding his trophy or medals.

The Home's rifle team was a member of the Western Ohio Junior Rifle League. Spectators were permitted to attend only by invitation. I was lucky enough to be invited to one meet when my boyfriend, Todd, was a member of the team. Held in the basement of the Home's Armory, I remember it being loud and exciting. Todd was a really good shooter. We won the meet and I was proud of our team, but especially thrilled that I had been invited to attend the meet with Todd.

Intramural basketball was a popular sport for the boys as they competed against the other vocational shops, for example, Auto vs Print shop. I think the prize to the winning shop was bragging rights for the whole next year.

Switchboard

"Good evening, OSSO Home." —Every switchboard operator at the Home

Another milestone. I was in tenth grade when I received my invitation to attend switchboard training. Many of the older girls were switchboard operators and they all seemed to love this assignment. I couldn't wait to start training.

The Home telephone system was directed through a two-cord, three-trunk line, one-person switchboard, located in the reception area of the Main Building. On weekdays Mrs. Stover, a full-time employee, was the main operator. High school girls, after passing a week-long training period, operated the switchboard in the evenings, on weekends, and on holidays when Mrs. Stover was off duty.

Our old OSSO Home switchboard now sits in our AXP Museum.

The actual switchboard sits today in our Museum located on the former Home grounds. There were about forty phone extensions around campus, and each was represented on the switchboard next to a little light and a plug. The three outside lines looked the same as the extensions. The Home phone numbers were 372-6908, 6909, and 6910. When calls came into the board from these outside lines, the light next to the corresponding ringing line lit up. We answered the call with a regular handset in one hand, and placed the left of the two cords into the lighted plug. We answered the call appropriately, "Good afternoon, OSSO Home," and answered general questions pertaining to the Home as appropriate.

If a call was received for an extension on campus we connected the call, but that could be tricky. Extensions around campus could call other extensions directly without passing through the switchboard. We operators had no good way of determining if an extension was already busy. All we could do was to grasp the right cord and gently place it near the plug of the extension to which we wanted to connect. If we detected a tiny bit of static, that meant the line was already busy. If no static was detected, we could connect the call. Sometimes it was hard to hear that little bit of static, and connecting resulted in placing a new call right into an existing conversation, making it a 3-person call. Folks tended not to appreciate having their calls interrupted that way, so we had to listen extremely carefully for the telltale static.

All outgoing calls from around campus, as well as all long distance calls, were placed through the switchboard. Calls were answered in the same manner using the left cord to answer and the right cord to connect. After the left cord was plugged in, a switch had to be flipped before the operator could be heard.

I enjoyed my turns at the switchboard. Although we were not paid for this assignment, I felt as though I were a grownup entrusted with great responsibility. I worked whenever I was scheduled, and was always happy to fill in for others when a substitute was needed. Switchboard assignment was a good chance to get out of the cottage and to chat with anyone who happened to drop by the Main Building. It could also be a quiet place to do homework in the evenings. I thought working on the switchboard was just fun.

Each morning the Officer of the Day (OD) was assigned to raise the flag in front of the Main Building, and then lower it in the evening. The rest of his time was normally spent being a presence and providing a sense of security at the Main Building. He would occasionally be called to help a supervisor with an unruly child. While working on the switchboard in the evenings and on weekends, it was fun to have the OD hanging around for company. I remember several little romances that sprang up between some of the switchboard operators and the Officers as a result of this hanging around the switchboard. The very few times when the stars lined up, and my boyfriend was OD while I was switchboard operator, he walked me back to my cottage at the end of my shift and gave me a quick goodnight kiss.

I was extra excited to be working the switchboard the evening of December 18, 1968. Jeannie was in labor and it was looking as if the baby would arrive soon. Loualtha promised that she would call me at the switchboard as soon as the baby arrived, but she definitely would call me before I left for the evening. Just before 9:00 p.m. when I would need to close down the switchboard, an outside call came in. I knew it had to be Loualtha calling about the baby.

I answered, "Good evening, OSSO Home," but there was no one on the other line.

Once again, "Good evening, OSSO Home," but still no one on the other end. And then, dial tone. Disappointment washed over me as I realized I had missed the call.

But soon the phone rang again and I again answered, "Good evening, OSSO Home." Still no one there.

I was getting frantic when I suddenly remembered the switch that must be flipped before I could be heard. I flipped the switch to hear the sweetest voice in the world announce that Baby Dean Philip Veneziano had arrived, and Mommy, Daddy, and Baby were all doing well!

I don't care what anyone says...I think having a baby is always hardest on the new auntie!

My first job after I graduated and left the Home was working as a switchboard operator at a large company. I was told that I was hired because I had switchboard experience. That switchboard, however, was nothing like the small one at the Home. This one filled a whole wall of a room with several stations and an operator at each one!

I really enjoyed all of my jobs, but if I had to pick the one that was the most fun, hands down it would be the switchboard. Computers have now eliminated the need for switchboards, so young people today will never have the opportunity I had to enjoy that experience.

Learning About Death

"Death is a distant rumor to the young." –Andrew A. Rooney

My first experience with death occurred when I was six years old. I had been in the Home for exactly one year, and my family could finally take the four of us home for a two-week vacation. But no one from my family came to pick us up. Instead, Loualtha and Joe's friends arrived to drive us home. My grandma had passed away the day before our scheduled visit.

I didn't exactly understand what was happening, but I knew something bad had happened to Grandma. Everyone seemed so sad. I felt as though I should be sad, too, but I really wasn't. I was just too happy getting away from the Home and being with my family again. The day of the funeral, Loualtha told us that we would not be going because she wanted us to "remember Grandma the way she was, not as she is now." I hadn't seen Grandma for a whole year. What was she like now?

Loualtha and Joe's neighbors spent the day of the funeral with the four of us and took us to the Village Inn for fried chicken. Deep inside, I was confused and frightened. What happened to Grandma? What was she like now?

When I was about the same age, Peter Pan children were bused to Sunday School at a church in downtown Xenia. The church was located next to a funeral home that we had to walk past to get to and from our parked bus. One of the kids in our group pointed out the funeral home and told us there were dead people inside. Some of the kids tried to peek in the windows, then ran away screaming. I was scared and ran past as quickly as I could, not even looking at the building.

I was in the fifth grade when my Jackson A cottage supervisor, Mrs. Hairopoulos, passed away from cancer. It was decided that all the girls in the cottage would attend the calling hours. I didn't want to go, but our feelings were not considered. We rode the Home bus to the funeral home. We were instructed to form a single line, walk past the casket, and keep right on walking out the door. We weren't to talk to anyone. Mrs. Hairopoulos was wearing a dark blue and white dress. There were sweet, fragrant flowers everywhere. I didn't look at her face. I walked as quickly as I could just to get out of there.

That evening was the beginning of a most uneasy time for me. I was afraid to be alone, afraid to go upstairs alone, and afraid to be in the basement alone. I couldn't make the fear go away, and I couldn't tell anyone. Who would understand? I didn't understand this fear myself.

When I was in ninth grade, there was a funeral in the Chapel. I was in Mrs. Lane's math class. We could see the Chapel from our classroom windows, could see the hearse parked out front, and people going into the service. We started asking Mrs. Lane questions about death and funerals. She stopped working on math and spent the rest of that class answering our questions. I appreciated Mrs. Lane's patience that day as we discussed death and dying instead of math.

It was spring, mere weeks before my high school graduation. Mr. and Mrs. Hartpence, the former Home superintendent and his wife, along with two other couples, were in a car accident on Easter Sunday. Mrs. Hartpence and the other four people died instantly. Mr. Hartpence died a few days later during his wife's funeral.

Rev. Howard took all the members of Church Council to the calling hours held at the Otterbein College Chapel in Westerville, Ohio. There were five caskets, more flowers than I've ever seen in one place, and hundreds of people. The caskets were closed. It was a relief that I didn't have to look at the people who had died. I didn't feel that scared feeling this time, but it didn't seem quite real to me. So many coffins, so many people.

When I was twenty-five, Loualtha died unexpectedly at sixty-one years of age. I experienced real grief for the first time. I wasn't afraid this time, just sad. In spite of my sadness, I was strong enough to give Joe the support he needed. Sadly six months later Joe passed away too, probably from a broken heart. He was eighty-one. He died on my twenty-sixth birthday.

Many aunts and uncles, several cousins and friends have died over the years. I truly started facing my own mortality a few years ago when my little brother, Jerry, passed away quite unexpectedly from a heart attack. He was 62. I wasn't prepared to lose him, had never even given it much thought. I guess I thought my siblings would be here with me for the whole ride through life. I tend to think about death more often nowadays, but am always hopeful for more time here on earth with my family.

Looking back, death was never explained to me in a loving, caring, healthy way. Maybe seeing my grandma would have lessened my fear of what she was like now. Perhaps being with family, seeing and understanding that death is a natural part of life, could have alleviated countless uneasy days for me. I would raise my own children in a way that I hope gave them a better understanding of death and spared them this fear that haunted me well into my adult life.

Learning About Money

"An investment in knowledge pays the best interest." –Benjamin Franklin

One of our favorite holiday events occurred early in November with a shopping trip to the JC Penney store in Xenia. Children were eligible to participate starting in 4th grade. We were scheduled by classroom during the school day to spend a couple of hours at the store. The Home bus picked us up in front of the school where we were each given a shopping bag and "scrip" (artificial money that was printed by students in the Home Print Shop) to buy ourselves a Christmas present. The amount of money each child received was based on age, and these dollar amounts had increased over the years. Children aged ten and under received $5.00; ages eleven–thirteen received $7.00; and ages fourteen and older received $10.00. As we checked out, our presents were labeled and taken away. We would not see them again until Christmas morning, beautifully wrapped, waiting for us under the Christmas tree in our cottage.

I don't remember if we had only one hour or two hours to spend our money, but I know I used every last second trying to decide what to buy. In my younger years, I headed straight to the toy department where I usually picked out a new doll baby. Choosing the perfect doll meant perusing every single doll in the store. My new doll had to be perfect, but also couldn't cost more than my allotted money.

As I reached my teens, clothes became more important to me than dolls. I tried to pick out a new blouse or dress while still saving some money to buy a stuffed animal or small toy. Eventually clothes were the only thing that interested me, and I tried to buy as much as I could with my hard earned scrip money.

Even though I picked out my own present, enough time passed that it still seemed like a surprise on Christmas morning, and every bit as special as any other gift that I received.

For several years after I moved to the main campus, we had a different kind of shopping spree at the SS Kresge 5-and-10-cent store to buy Christmas presents for our families. These trips were made in the evening after dinner, boys one evening and girls the next.

The year I remember best, my siblings and I each had a set amount of scrip money. My guess is that we each had about $5.00 to spend. Rick took charge and made a list of every single relative including our mom, aunts, uncles and cousins that we would see over the Christmas holiday. He split the list into two, giving Jeannie and me half while keeping the other half for himself and Jerry. Our assignment was to buy a little present for every single person on the list with our combined money. There were nine aunts and uncles, my mom, and several cousins.

We were beyond proud of ourselves the day of our family Christmas party when we gave every single person a small present. The only gifts I still remember giving were a perfume and powder set to my mother, and a tube of bright red lipstick to my Aunt Barbara—a gift I just knew she would love. My younger cousin Lauri recently told me she still has her powder puff set, and how thrilled she was to receive it from us.

I was sixteen the year that I had already decided I was getting a new Easter outfit even before Loualtha and Joe had arrived for their visit. That was the year Loualtha told us we could go to the store, but they were a little short on money. We could each buy something for a dollar, but they just couldn't afford to buy Easter outfits. I did not react nicely at all.

"I need a new outfit," I proclaimed.

Loualtha explained again that they were a little short on money this time, and she just couldn't afford to buy me something. But I had already told my friends I was getting a new outfit. And I pouted until she gave in. We went to Rinks Department Store where Loualtha told me I could pick out an inexpensive outfit. I selected a bright yellow skirt and top set. It cost only a few dollars, but it was pretty, and I had some bright yellow earrings to wear with the outfit.

As I summarize for myself the lessons I learned during these memorable shopping sprees...

In the JC Penney Store story, I was handed scrip money to spend on myself. I enjoyed picking out a present and enjoyed opening it on Christmas morning. I remember the fun of shopping, of learning to stay within the allocated amount I was given, but I honestly don't remember any specific thing I bought.

In the Kresge Store story, we were buying for others. We were again given scrip money, we had a lot of fun shopping, and were required to stay within our allocated amount. But these presents were for others, not for ourselves. Even though the gifts were really inexpensive, I remember trying incredibly hard to pick out something that each person would love. And over fifty years later, I still remember what two of my relatives received. I remember the excitement I felt wrapping each of their presents. And I will never forget the joy and pride I felt as those presents were handed out and opened. Hearing that our gift meant so much to at least one cousin brings all those good feelings back to me. I learned that, for me, it is definitely better to give than to receive.

As for the Easter outfit, it was nice, but I never felt good about myself in it. I was glad Loualtha bought me the outfit, but ashamed of myself for the way I treated her that day. I think I learned a better lesson by my aunt buying the outfit she couldn't really afford than if she had said no and stuck to her guns. I learned to not ask others for money or gifts. I learned to not question another's finances. I learned to not beg for things when I've been told "no." And I'm very thankful I didn't have to see what my aunt had to give up in order to balance her budget that week.

I don't remember very many of my Easter outfits, but I will never forget this one which is shown on the back cover of this book.

You Know You're a
Home Girl if...

1. You still gulp your food to be sure your mouth isn't full when the dessert chimes are rung and you have to serve—on the boy's side.
2. You know how heavy a white metal basket with a vicious spike, full of peonies (with an army of ants) is.
3. You see a green field with a lot of uniformed guys when you hear Stars and Stripes Forever.
4. Peter Pan does not evoke Tinkerbell, but a lot of tiny chairs and tables to set.
5. You tend to circle to the left when you ride a bike.
6. When you hear a steam whistle, you are inclined to change tasks.
7. You can still identify the sound of breaking hair when you walked from the gym in winter.
8. You can change shirts in public without showing anything.

9. When someone recites *In Flanders Fields*, you wonder why they don't put the proper emphasis on the right spots.
10. Musical boyfriends was a teenage reality game.
11. You're still checking for wolf spiders in your laundry room.
12. You still wash whites first—even though you no longer have to use the same water over again.
13. You call/ed your child "young lady" or "young man" when you're mad—even though you SWORE you wouldn't.
14. You finally figured out who that 2-hour nap time was really for (and don't you wish you had time for them now).
15. When you're doing charity work, you can't help but wonder if you're turning into a big bosomed Gold Star mother.
16. You're really good at cleaning—one room, for a month. And move on to the next room the next month.
17. You would never, ever, never buy a pair of saddle shoes.
18. It took you years to figure out how to cook meat correctly.
19. You feel guilty if you don't baste before sewing—and you always use a thimble.
20. Deferred gratification is not in your vocabulary.
21. You just can't, even after all these years, stack another book on top of a Bible.
22. And you really know you're a Home girl if you think things are nice to have but you would share anything with a friend.

—Kathy Trnka Camarena
OSSO Home, Class of 1967
Used with Permission

The Chapel

*"I like the silent church before the service begins,
better than any preaching." –Ralph Waldo Emerson*

Collier Chapel was our non-denominational church situated near the front gates of the Home. This beautiful brick building was the central focus of our religious life. All Home children who lived on the main campus attended Sunday morning services there. The only exception was for Catholic children who were bused to St. Brigid Catholic Church in Xenia.

Upon entering the Chapel, a sign inside the door greeted us with the words, "Enter to Worship," and a gentle reminder upon exiting, "Depart to Serve."

Cottages were seated in assigned rows as always, boys on one side and girls on the other. Supervisors sat with their cottage group to make sure there was no nonsense in church.

Our Chaplain was Rev. Howard, and he was my favorite employee at the Home. Although our Chapel was non-denominational, Rev. Howard was ordained as a Methodist minister. His sermons were always short and interesting, geared toward teenagers and infused with humorous little anecdotes.

A retired minister occasionally filled in for Rev. Howard while he was on vacation. One memorable Sunday, this substitute minister was standing behind the pulpit busily preaching hell, fire and brimstone. The choir was sitting directly behind the good reverend when he suddenly threw up his hands as if to say, "Praise the Lord!" and his pants fell down! He didn't miss a beat as he reached down and pulled them right back up, mumbling something to the effect, "Well, these things happen." I don't believe anyone in the congregation even realized what had just happened, but those of us in the choir couldn't miss it.

Being a typical teenage girl, I wanted to laugh, but I couldn't risk the trouble it would have caused me. But next to me, Jeannie was shaking like a bowl full of jelly. I could feel her whole body tremble as she tried to not laugh out loud, and I started giggling inside, too. Soon tears were rolling down both

Jeannie and I in our choir robes in front of Collier Chapel shortly before Jeannie graduated.

of our cheeks as we tried to choke back our giggles. We didn't dare make eye contact or it would have been all over for us. We somehow made it through to the end of the service. Once in the choir room, many of us laughed until we cried. Some of the choir members did not think the incident was funny at all, and they admonished us sternly.

Our choir visited several other churches throughout the year. We presented a concert for those congregations, and were usually treated to dinner or dessert.

I particularly remember traveling to the First Baptist Church in Ironton, Ohio. Because of the distance, we were invited to spend the night as guests in the homes of church members. Jeannie and I stayed at the same residence. We were treated to a homemade breakfast before returning to the Home. We had fun on the return bus ride comparing the various breakfasts that were served to us. Jeannie and I had bacon, eggs, toast, and fruit—just a wonderful breakfast—as were most. Except for one boy who complained that he was served, as he called it, sticky-in-the-throat oatmeal. Everyone on the bus laughed at his misfortune, and I was happy that we hadn't stayed where he had!

Rev. Howard taught Confirmation Class for 7th–8th grade students who were interested in joining the Church. Those who successfully passed this

Jeannie's Wedding—
Rev. Howard, Jeannie
and new husband,
Phil Veneziano.

My family at Jeannie's wedding—Jerry, our mother, Bernice, me,
Rick and his wife, Jeannie and Phil.

class was baptized and confirmed on Easter Sunday. Each year a group of ten to twenty students was baptized. I successfully passed this class, and was baptized by Rev. Howard.

Rev. Howard also taught a Religious Education class to grades six through nine as part of the school curriculum. This required class met weekly for one period, and covered Old Testament Times; Protestant Heritage; Hebrew Kings, Prophets and People; and Christ's Life and Ours. I'm not sure how much of this information I retained. I know Rev. Howard tried to make the class interesting, but I remember that I found it pretty boring.

The Chapel's governing body was the Church Council, a group of twelve elected student Chapel members who met monthly. Newly confirmed members were welcomed into the Chapel by these members. Prayers in the main dining room could be led only by a member of Church Council. I was honored to be a member of this group during my sophomore, junior and senior years of high school, where I served as Treasurer my last two years.

Two confirmation students were assigned by Church Council to serve as acolytes each week. I took my turns during my confirmation year. We wore black robes and marched down the aisle before the service started, to light the altar candles, and then again put out the candles at the end of the service.

Communion was never served during Sunday morning services. Rather it was held once a month on Sunday evenings, and was open only to Church members. Because Mr. Gunn did not attend this evening service, an organ student provided the music. I took piano lessons for many years, and switched to organ in the 11th grade. As a member of Church Council, I was asked to play for Communion services, and I did for two years as a junior and senior. But I had learned only one song well enough to play on the organ at these services. So I played "Just as I am Without One Plea" over and over at the beginning and end of the service, as well as during the time Communion was being served.

Students from nearby Cedarville College helped Rev. Howard facilitate the voluntary Youth Fellowship program which met for two hours on three Sunday evenings per month. Because this was such a popular activity and almost everyone participated, the participants were divided into three groups: 6th, 7th, and 8th; 9th and 10th; 11th and 12th. Each week, one group met in the Chapel for devotions and singing. One group met in the gym for short devotions followed by open gym and swimming. The last group met in the Orfenz Den for short devotions and games. The groups rotated so that everyone could enjoy each activity once a month.

These same Cedarville College students ran our Sunday School program that met in the Auditorium and school building. Younger children on main campus were required to attend each week. Once in high school, we could choose for ourselves whether or not to participate. I remember that I attended most weeks.

Many former students came back to have Rev. Howard marry them in our Chapel. My sister Jeannie and her husband Phil Veneziano were married in the Chapel on January 20, 1968. I was her Maid of Honor, Uncle Joe gave her away, and Rick and Jerry were ushers. It was a simple but beautiful ceremony. It meant a lot to Jeannie and our family to have Rev. Howard officiate her wedding at our Chapel.

Military Training

"Sound off, one two; Sound off, three four; Cadence count,
one two three four, one two … three four." –Orphan boys during drills

Although girls did not participate at all in military training, at least during my years in the Home, all boys 7th grade and above were required to join the Home's military program. I feel it is important for me to include some details about this program as it generated a regimented atmosphere for all of us.

From 1927 until the fall of 1967, the Home operated a military-type program, the National Defense Cadet Corps (NDCC). This program was unique to the Home, financed by the State of Ohio, both designed and taught academically at the Home. Col. Herman Gill managed this program during the years I was in the Home. The uniforms were blue and gray with Eisenhower style jackets.

In 1968, the program transitioned to a junior Reserve Officer Training Corp (ROTC) for boys in 9th through 12th grades. This program was mostly funded by the federal government with instruction provided by the Army, who also provided uniforms, books and weapons. The Home instituted and funded a pre-ROTC program for boys in the 7th and 8th grades. The new uniforms were Army green but with blue lapels, differentiating them from regular Army uniforms.

Boys in 9th through 12th grades were required to take a Military Science Class. This graded class met once each week and practiced each weekday at noon. The boys were taught military discipline, military courtesy, military history, and parade and drill. After completing this four-year course, boys who entered the Army after graduation were automatically granted a private first-class rank.

The Battalion was made up of three companies, A, B and the Band, and was headed by a student Major and his Adjutant. By the time they graduated,

Rick and Jerry were both officers in the band. Each of the three Companies were led by a Captain who was usually a senior boy, and each of the Companies was comprised of two Platoons, each commanded by a Lieutenant. The Majors, Captains and Lieutenants were officers and carried sabers. Each Company also had a First Sergeant who marched at the rear of the Company and carried only a pistol (not loaded). Each Platoon was comprised of four Squads, each led by a Sergeant. There were eight to ten Privates and Corporals in each Squad. Each Sergeant, Corporal and Private carried an M-1 rifle. Boys on main campus but not yet twelve years old were assigned to a group called Rookies. They learned the Manual of Arms and marching drills with fake rifles called 'dummies.'

A Federal Inspection was held each year. Our battalion regularly earned "Honor School Rating." The boys were released from school for the entire day while we girls still had to attend in the morning. In the afternoon, a movie was shown in the auditorium for the girls and any children too young to participate in the military exercises.

The 40 et 8 sponsored a Field Day each spring. The two military companies (A and B) competed for a saber awarded to the winning Captain. This fairly intense competition took several hours to complete and involved squad drills, platoon drills, and company drills. Individual drills followed with cash prizes awarded to the winner. After the competitions were over, all of the Home kids met at the football field for sack races, tug-of-war, hurdling, and running races with cash prizes awarded to the winners. Some of the 40 et 8 chapters brought their boxcars to campus, and this was when they gave rides to the younger children.

The Military Ball was held that evening, complete with a live band provided by the 40 et 8. The Officers and their dates paraded into the Ball under a saber arch and then danced the first dance. A Queen of the Ball was elected each year and announced during the dance. My senior year I ran for queen, but lost to my friend Joanne who was elected Queen of the Ball. A special dance was held for the queen and her court. Joanne's boyfriend was the winning Captain that day, making this an extra special evening for both of them.

A weekly highlight for the entire Home was the Sunday afternoon Retreat Parade, when the band led the two military companies onto the parade field. The band played *The Stars and Stripes Forever* as the two companies marched

Jerry and Rick in their older military uniforms.

onto the field. The band then played *El Capitan* as it marched in front of the companies. Both companies presented arms, and the flag was lowered as the band played *The Star Spangled Banner*. The battalion commanders then drilled their companies in the Manual of Arms. The parade was completed by a Pass in Review.

All of the Home children attended this ceremony. Sunday visitors to the Home usually included it in their visit. Even Xenia residents occasionally dropped by to watch this impressive ceremony.

Between April and June, both military companies marched to and from Chapel each Sunday with the band leading the way.

I believe this military training was a good thing. Our boys were well behaved, and they all had good manners. I felt proud when I was with my brothers or a boyfriend in uniform. It was so much nicer than blue jeans! I'm also happy that we girls didn't have to participate. Shortly after I graduated and left the Home, it became a requirement for girls to also participate in ROTC.

Dating

"The beautiful thing about young love is the truth
in our hearts that it will last forever." –Atticus

I can't hear the song *Bobby's Girl* by Marcia Blane without thinking of Bobby, my little boyfriend in elementary school, who was a sweet, red-haired cutie. We always said we were boyfriend and girlfriend, but that's as far as it went. We were both a little shy and I'm not sure we even spoke much to each other.

As I got older and progressed through junior high and high school, having a boyfriend seemed rather important to me, as it seemed to be for many of the other girls in the Home. I'm not sure if it was a status symbol, peer pressure, or maybe just reassurance that someone cared about us.

Skip became my boyfriend around 7th grade, and we liked each other off and on through 10th grade. We were not old enough to really date in the beginning, but it was fun to have a boyfriend to smile at, wave to, and think about.

Harold was in 10th grade, two years older than me and Rick's good friend. While I was too young to officially date, I was able to invite him to my spring piano recital, and he kissed me afterward...my first kiss! Harold gave me his picture and a 45-rpm record that played *You're the One* by The Vogues. Shortly after, he dumped me for another girl. I was heartbroken and humiliated, as he asked me for his picture and record back so he could give them to the other girl who just happened to live in my same cottage. My self-confidence took a nosedive as I worried about what was wrong with me.

The Home had rules to cover just about any situation, and they were spelled out in black and white with few, if any, gray areas. I believe this was a good thing. Sure, I didn't like all the rules, but I did like the security that comes from knowing and understanding what was expected of me, and more important, what I could expect as I grew into the next age group. I will never forget The Dating Rules. Supervised dating was allowed, with permission from both the girl's supervisor as well as the boy's supervisor, when both the boy and the girl were at least fifteen years old and in the 9th grade.

Having an October birthday, I was one of the first girls in my class to turn fifteen and be eligible to date. Of course, the first boy I officially dated was Skip. He was cute, extremely smart, and sweet. My supervisor, Mrs. Purtell, loved him to pieces, and I never had to worry about getting her permission to date him. Our date planning started early in the week when Skip walked over to my cottage to ask Mrs. Purtell if he could take me to the Saturday night movie.

Sometime during my high school years, a new dating procedure was added. Now Dating Cards were required. Everyone eligible to date was issued a card. When a boy asked a girl's supervisor for permission to have a date, he presented this card. That way the girl's supervisor knew the boy was eligible to date. Girls rarely needed to use their Dating Card except to have it taken away at the whim of the supervisor or dean. Any student on detention lost his or her Dating Card for that week.

A Saturday evening movie was held each week without fail. All the children on main campus were required to attend with their cottages and supervisors, except for those on detention. Each cottage group sat in assigned rows, girls on one side and boys on the other, *He gave me a diamond promise ring and asked me to marry him.* with younger cottages toward the front and older cottages in the back. Dating couples walked to the auditorium with the girl's cottage group, and sat next to her supervisor. Couples were permitted to hold hands during the movies but nothing more. After the movie, the couple walked back to the girl's cottage where they were permitted to kiss goodnight at the front door. They could linger there until the girl's supervisor turned the porch light on and off to signal that it was time for the boy to leave. Skip and I dated through most of 9th and part of 10th grades. I don't remember why we broke up because I really liked him. I do remember that as well as being sad, I was also pretty angry with him at the time.

I was dating Cliff at the beginning of my senior year when a new girl, Kathy, entered the Home. She was homesick and lonely. Remembering how I had felt the same way when I first came to the Home, I asked Cliff to be nice to her and to ask his friends to be nice to her, too. Cliff took my advice to heart and was extremely nice to her. So nice that before long he broke up with me to date her. They dated all through our senior year and he eventually married her. Kathy and I remained friends, and a few years later I was a bridesmaid in their wedding.

Todd was a year older than me, and was my off-again, on-again boyfriend for a couple years, starting in 10th grade. Todd was a true orphan with no family outside of the Home. He graduated the year before I did and was invited to live with an employee and her family in Xenia. He visited me quite often at the Home and made it a point to attend all our Home football games and sporting events so we could see each other. He brought me a single rose twice each week, one red and one yellow. At Christmas of my senior year, he gave me a diamond promise ring and asked me to marry him. I excitedly agreed to marry Todd, but we would wait until we were a little older. At Christmas, I spent the week with Loualtha and Joe. They threw a fit over my diamond ring and insisted I return it. I sadly gave it back. I loved Todd, but knew we were too young. Respecting my aunt's wishes, I broke up with him.

After Todd and I broke up, I did not date seriously again in high school. Instead I hung out the rest of the senior year with my best girlfriends—Joanne, Phyllis, and Kathy. I started dating Stan who was truly "just a friend." We had the best times without the stress of labeling it a relationship. We went to movies, prom, and other senior activities together.

One Saturday evening I had a date with "just a friend" Stan. My friend Phyllis had a date with another guy in our class, Matt. Matt was a good friend, but we had never dated. This particular Saturday, Matt talked Stan into switching dates with him, but without telling us girls. So, Matt came to pick me up, and Stan picked up Phyllis. I was pretty annoyed with this surprise, but grudgingly went along with it. Looking back, I've always wished I had just laughed and enjoyed the date. We were all friends, and it was actually a pretty funny gag.

Besides Saturday movies, dating couples who were at least sixteen could also attend dances, class, and cottage parties, and special parties for groups such as band, rifle, and drama. Sometimes other special dating activities were enjoyed. Dating couples were allowed to "promenade," meaning they could walk together for an hour or two around the large parade field on Sunday afternoons. The couples could hold hands as they walked together and sometimes managed to even sneak in a little kiss. Occasionally one of the Deans would allow a special promenade on a summer evening. I once talked Rev. Howard into inviting Church Council members to visit in the Teachers' Lounge on a Sunday evening when there were no other activities. He stayed in his office across the hall. During my senior year, Church Council was comprised of mostly dating couples. We loved this event and considered it a special date.

Couples at the Home seemed to follow a set of established dating rituals. It was mandatory that couples acknowledge each other in the dining room. This was usually a wave and hello from across the large room, followed by several smiles and glances throughout the meal. And, woe to the fellow who walked out of the dining room without a good-bye wave and a smile for his girl. Between classes at school, most couples tried to walk together, and hand-holding was permitted. Stealing kisses in the stairwell was known to happen but, if caught, could result in detention for the couple.

One of our weirdest dating rituals occurred during summers on the playground. Both boys and girls were required to be outside on the playground from 6:30–9:00 p.m. The two playgrounds were about 160 yards apart with an open field separating them. Many couples spent those evenings engaging in our strange dating ritual—waving across the field to each other all evening long.

Both boys and girls were busy swinging, riding bicycles, playing tether ball, 4-square, and board games, but the softball fields were the best location on the playgrounds for maximum view of the opposite sex, and the best location for waving. Cottage teams played intramural softball for a cottage championship at the end of the summer. Boys were expected to wave right before batting, at each base as they progressed, and after they reached home base. If they made an out, that was also good for a wave. We girls behaved similarly. There were some girls who didn't even play softball—they just stood and waved. I tried that a few times, but it was boring and my arm eventually got tired. Softball was way more fun. When the 9:00 p.m. CQ whistle blew, signaling time to go in, the waving and blowing kisses intensified. I don't know who started this ritual, but I almost wish they hadn't!

After social events, couples were permitted to walk together as far as The Corner. At The Corner these couples were allowed to kiss goodnight. The Dean of Girls, the Dean of Boys, or the Chaplain was right there to supervise and to determine when it was time to move on.

Following a brief breakup period, Cliff and I got back together at a dance, and he walked me to The Corner. He kissed me goodnight, and as he walked away he pulled out his shirt tail. Cliff hated to tuck in his shirt and he always pulled it out as soon as he could get away with it. Well, Ms. Henize, the Dean of Girls, was supervising The Corner that evening. She saw us kiss and watched as he untucked his shirt. She walked right up to him and demanded his Dating Card. The next day I was called to her office.

"I need you to come to my office, and bring your Dating Card," read the note I received from Ms. Henize.

I slowly walked to her office, wondering what I could have possibly done to warrant her wanting my Dating Card.

As I handed her my card, she explained. "You caused Cliff to get so excited that he had to untuck his shirt to hide his excitement, and I know you understand what I mean. I'm taking away both of your Dating Cards for the rest of the time you are in the Home," she concluded.

I was too embarrassed to respond to her accusation. It seemed silly to me because nothing had happened at The Corner other than a goodnight kiss. I also knew that Cliff just hated to tuck in his shirt. I don't recall ever seeing my Dating Card again, but somehow I still was able to date, as was Cliff.

Sex was never an issue for me in high school, and I don't think it was an issue for my friends either. Holding hands, waving, hugging, and kissing was as far as it ever went for me with any Home boy. Anything further never occurred to me, and I assume it never occurred to the boys I dated either. I can't say that sex never happened between Home students because I know of at least two girls who were sent away because they were pregnant. I don't know where they were sent or whether they received any kind of help from the Home. Neither one ever returned.

Many former Home kids ended up getting married to other Home kids. It seems that many of those marriages didn't last; however some have stood the test of time. I imagine these couples share a special bond due to both being raised in the Home, but they were also raised with an obvious lack of a good role model. Both of my brothers married girls from the Home. Neither marriage lasted. My sister and I both married men from outside of the Home. My sister married the first man she met after knowing him for only two months. They raised five children, and recently celebrated their 50th wedding anniversary. I married a friend of my family. I didn't know him well when we started dating, but did know his mother and brother. We dated for a year before we were married. We divorced after 19 years. I'm glad we did get married, though, because we have three beautiful children and ten beautiful grandchildren. I wouldn't change that for anything in the world. I'm currently happily married to another 'outsider.'

Saturday Night Movies

"I feel there is no substitute for going out to the movies. There is nothing like it!" –Steven Spielberg

Saturday evenings meant movie night in the auditorium. While in Peter Pan, we went only to shows that would interest small children. When we did get to go, we sat right up front in the very first rows. I stared up at the huge red velvet curtain that covered the screen. At the center top were the initials "WW."

I asked, "Mommy Carmen, what does "WW" mean?"

At least one little girl asked this question every single time we went to the movies. I now know it stood for Woodrow Wilson, our high school name.

Mommy Carmen laughingly answered, "It stands for Wiggle Worms because you girls never sit still."

I enjoyed hearing Mommy Carmen laugh as she called us wiggle worms. We all laughed when she said it.

Once in Pan 7, we were able to attend the Saturday night movies more often. When we had misbehaved in the cottage and really shouldn't have been allowed to attend, but had to go with the rest of the cottage, Mommy Rebecca had a special punishment for us. We were required to put cotton balls in our ears and keep our head down so we couldn't see or hear the movie. This happened to me once or twice. Because we were right up front, I could hear the movie clearly, and I kept peeking at the screen. I once got caught looking up and received a quick smack on the head. Whoops!

A cartoon was shown before every movie. Some of the classics we saw were *Mickey Mouse, The Roadrunner, Precious the Dog, Nancy, Popeye the Sailor Man, Bugs Bunny, Mighty Mouse, Porky Pig, Tom & Jerry, Woody Woodpecker, Casper the Friendly Ghost, Mr. Magoo,* and *Yogi Bear.*

Many of our movies were westerns with cowboys or films about World War II. It seemed that we saw every single Rory Calhoun movie ever made, many John Wayne movies, and the inside of every single submarine used in the war. War movies and westerns weren't my favorites, but I remember that the boys seemed to enjoy them. I liked comedies and family movies. These are some of the movies I remember seeing on Saturday evenings in the Auditorium. I know there were many, many others.

My Favorite Movies:
Bye, Bye, Birdie
Follow Me Boys
Little Shepherd of Kingdom Come
Music Man
Oklahoma
Pollyanna
Shenandoah
Spencer's Mountain
State Fair
That Darn Cat
The Inn of the Sixth Happiness
The Parent Trap
The Robe
Trouble with Angels

Other Movies I Remember Seeing:
A Dog of Flanders
Absent Minded Professor
Air Patrol
Apache Uprising
Battle of the Coral Sea
Barabbas
Beau Geste
Black Spurs
Critic's Choice

Donovan's Reef
Don't Give Up the Ship
Family Jewels
Follow that Dream
Ghost and Mr. Chicken
Guns of Navarone
Hercules
Horse Soldiers
Jumbo
Old Yeller
Pocket Full of Miracles
Roman Holiday
The Secret of Monte Christo
Seven Days in May
Shaggy Dog
The Sons of Katie Elder
Texas Across the River
The Appaloosa
The Birds
The Big Fisherman
The Flying Fontaine
The Plainsman
The War Wagon
Toby Tyler
The Ugly Dachshund
Voyage to the Bottom of the Sea
Who's Minding the Store?

I believe that overall we were treated to a nice selection of movies, even if it seemed like too many westerns and war movies for me. Our movies were funded by the state, and chosen by the administration. The only thing missing was popcorn!

Dances

I Could Have Danced All Night." –Alan Jay Lerner

Wallflower: A person who, because of shyness, unpopularity, or lack of a partner, remains at the side at a party or dance. Or a person who just 'doesn't do dancing.' That was me. Feeling as though I didn't really know how to dance at all. I especially didn't like to fast dance, and survived most of our dances by slow dancing. I enjoyed attending dances and other social events; it was just the actual dancing that caused me distress.

Luckily for me, most of our dances back then were slow and provided the opportunity to snuggle up with my partner. My favorite song for slow dancing, one that seemed to bring everyone to the dance floor, was *Unchained Melody* by the Righteous Brothers. Popular fast dances back then were the Bunny Hop, the Twist, the Freddie, the Loco-Motion, the Mashed Potato, the Shimmy, the Swim, the Watusi, the Limbo and the Monkey. My favorite of these was the Freddie. It was a simple dance, and even those who didn't dance too well could join in. While giving a little hop, you raised your right arm and leg, then your left arm and leg. It was the simplest way to have fun when everyone else was fast dancing.

Several dances were held throughout the year for students in high school, including Back-to-School, Homecoming, New Year's Eve, Valentine's Day, St. Patrick's Day, Sadie Hawkins, and the Junior-Senior Prom. We wore our Sunday best clothing to most of the dances, which were held in the Orfenz Den with music provided by our social studies teacher, Mr. Might. He was full of energy, loved us Home kids, and cherished his opportunity to DJ our dances. He owned great sound equipment and a large collection of popular music. We usually had pop and chips to snack on during the evening. Dances usually lasted two or three hours, ending by 11:00 p.m., except the New Year's Eve dance that ended at midnight. Home employees, mostly teachers, volunteered to chaperone our dances, and once in a while they even danced, too.

Senior Prom 1969. My date and I with Jerry and his date.

The Back-to-School dance was sponsored by the Association of Ex-Pupils. They provided a live band and a large variety of refreshments. The Military Ball was sponsored by the Officers' Wives Club from nearby Wright-Patterson Air Force Base. These wonderful ladies provided a live band as well as refreshments throughout the evening. They usually served cold cut sandwiches, chips, pop, and homemade baked goodies.

In the summertime high school students attended street dances which, as the name implies, were dances held outside in the street. The summer before ninth grade, I attended a street dance. It was my very first dance. The loud music for these dances was also provided by Mr. Might. Lights were strung through the trees along the dance area. I wore a black skirt with boxed pleats and a summery white blouse. Jeannie taught me to polish my white tennis shoes and explained that all the really cool girls wore cinnamon colored hosiery with their clean, white tennis shoes. So that's what I wore, too.

The Sadie Hawkins dance, named after a *Li'l Abner* cartoon character, was special because the girls asked the guys to be their dates, and also asked them to dance. I would ask boys to dance with me, but I found asking a boy for a date was a bit intimidating. What if he said no? Unless I had a definite boyfriend at the time, I never asked anyone to be my date for this dance. I came to understand how boys must feel whenever they ask a girl out. It takes a certain amount of courage.

Two formal dances were held each year: the Junior-Senior Prom and the Military Ball, discussed earlier in the Military Training chapter. The prom was hosted by the Junior class, which earned money throughout the year by sponsoring several fund raisers such as candy sales, car washes, and newspaper recycling to help pay for the costs associated with the evening. All juniors and seniors were invited to attend the prom. Students in lower grades were not permitted to attend even if they had a 'significant other' attending. For my junior year, we hosted a two-night event for the senior class. The first night was an all-night party at Wright-Patterson Air Force Base. We were given full use of their gym, swimming pool, and bowling lanes. The Officers' Wives Club provided refreshments throughout the evening. The second night we hosted the seniors to a delicious dinner at David's Buffet in Dayton, followed by the movie *Around the World in 80 Days* at the Salem Mall Cinema, also located in Dayton.

For my senior prom, the junior class hosted my class to a dinner and dance held on campus in the Orfenz Den. The Den was beautifully decorated in a Japanese Garden theme. At midnight following the dance, the movie, *The Thomas Crown Affair*, was shown upstairs in the auditorium.

We girls wore beautiful gowns while most of the boys wore suits. Some of the senior boys, including my date, were unhappy that the prom was held on the Home grounds rather than off-campus as in previous years. These boys rebelled by wearing blue jeans and t-shirts. I was mortified when my date came to pick me up in that casual attire. And to make matters worse, graduation was the next day, so Loualtha and Joe were already in town and they showed up to take prom pictures. Jerry wore a sharp new suit. He looked handsome in the pictures as did his date Brenda. And there was my date Stan in his blue jeans and t-shirt. I felt embarrassed all dressed up standing next to Stan. Shortly after the dance started I quickly ran back to my cottage and changed out of my gown into a short, more casual dress. I was seething inside at Stan and all the guys who had dressed that way, but it was my prom and my last night in the Home. I made the best of it and really did have a wonderful evening.

Whenever there was an upcoming formal dance, the Dean of Girls opened up a room in the main building that was full of party dresses and gowns. She invited us to go through them and pick out something to wear. These used dresses were donated to the Home mostly by veterans' organizations or the Association of Ex-Pupils. Many of the dresses in that room were pretty outdated, but we could always manage to find something presentable to wear.

Jeannie graduated the summer before my junior year. She had a job, and during my family summer vacation, took me shopping and bought me a beautiful yellow formal gown, complete with shoes, gloves, and hosiery. One of my best friends, Phyllis, had an older sister too, who bought her a lovely pink gown with accessories. Our Dean of Girls, Ms. Henize, had a rule that no new gowns could be worn to the prom or the Military Ball—only hand-me-downs. She said it would make the girls who didn't have a new gown feel bad. She told me and Phyllis specifically that we could not wear our new gowns that year. We didn't understand her reasoning, and we both decided to wear our new gowns to the Military Ball anyway. Of course Ms. Henize was a chaperone at the dance. She took one look at us and sent us back to our cottage to change. The next year just before the Military Ball, Ms. Henize told us that we could now wear our gowns because they weren't new anymore, but a year old. That seemed like stupid logic to me, but I was just happy to be able to wear my beautiful dress. And then, when the prom rolled around, Phyllis and I swapped dresses. She wore my yellow gown and I wore her pink one, gowns that were still new and beautiful a year later.

Singing

"My heart is like a singing bird." –Christina Rossetti

Music and singing were two of my passions at the Home, and many of the songs I learned there have stayed with me throughout my life. These are the songs I have sung over and over to my children and grandchildren. It seems as though we had a song for nearly every occasion.

On Sunday morning in Chapel, I can still hear Rev. Howard leading us in the singing of old traditional hymns. Some of my favorites were *A Mighty Fortress is Our God*, *Faith of Our Fathers*, and *The Church's One Foundation*. I loved hearing Rev. Howard's deep voice as he led us in singing these old hymns. I still like to play them on the piano, and enjoy them again and again.

Easter morning brought special resurrection songs, and the choir sang my favorite Easter hymn, *One Early Easter Morning*.

Memorial Day was one of our most cherished days of the year, as we honored children who had died while students at the Home. We celebrated their lives with a solemn parade, flowers, flags, and songs. Not a Memorial Day passes for me without remembering our beautiful celebration at the Home. At the cemetery we sang a song written by one of our teachers, placing flowers on the word *deck* and the flags on the word *flag*.

Flowers that are springing, mosses that are clinging,
Garlands we are bringing to deck these mounds today.
These are but a token. They are cherished still,
Who in sleep unbroken these narrow houses fill.
Though in silence sleeping, though fond hearts are weeping,
Watches still we're keeping o'er our country's flag.
For their great devotion, will forever live.
Folks can never trample upon the rights they give.

The girls in choir sang another special song, *Cover Them Over with Beautiful Flowers* by Theodore Wood.

Graduation was the most bittersweet day at the Home. Graduates were leaving and looking forward to starting new lives, but were sad at the thought of leaving siblings and dear friends behind. It was also sad for those left behind as they watched their loved one drive away. And of course, we had a song, *The Future*.

Oh I often sit and wonder, when the sun is sinking low,
Where shall yonder future find me, does but God in Heaven know?
Shall I be among the living? Shall I be among the free?
Where so ere my pathway leads me, Savior keep my heart with thee.
Oh the future lies before me, and I know not where I'll be.
But where ere my pathway leads me, Savior keep my heart with thee.

But perhaps my work for Jesus soon in future may be done.
All my earthly trials ended, and my crown in Heaven won.
Then forever with the ransomed, through eternity I'll be
Chanting hymns to him who bought me,
With his blood shed on a tree.

Oh the future lies before me, and I know not where I'll be.
But where ere my pathway leads me, Savior keep my heart with thee.
—A. A. Armen, Jennie Stout, 1884

Of course, we started each sporting event with our national anthem, *The Star-Spangled Banner*, yet another song I learned at the Home. Sporting events also found us singing a few special cheers/songs.

We're from Wilson, mighty, mighty Wilson
Everywhere we go people want to know
Who we are, so we tell them
We're from Wilson, mighty, mighty Wilson...

My first Christmas morning in Peter Pan, I heard our own *Home Christmas Carol* for the first time. This song soon became my favorite, and remains to this day, my most cherished Christmas Carol. It was written in the late 1800s especially for Home children by Sara E. Collins, a music teacher at the Home.

Wish you Merry Christmas
Hark the joyous song
How the richest voices
Roll the notes along
Happy hearts responding
To the welcome call
Wish you Merry Christmas
Merry Christmas All!
Let your sweetest numbers flow
Wake the Heavenly song again
Sung by angels long ago
Peace on earth
Good will toward men.

Wish you Merry Christmas
Merry Christmas all
May the richest blessings
Ever on you fall
Every year be brighter
Than the one before
And your Christmas mornings
Many, many more!

Let your sweetest numbers flow
Wake the Heavenly song again
Sung by angels long ago
Peace on earth
Good will toward men!

Merry, merry, merry, merry, merry, merry, merry, merry
Merry, merry Christmas all!
Merry, merry, merry, merry, merry, merry, merry, merry
Merry, merry Christmas all!
Merry, merry, merry, merry, merry, merry, merry, merry
Merry, merry Christmas all!

This song brings many happy memories of Christmases long ago when the carolers woke me up as a young Peter Pan child; and later as we carolers woke up the younger Peter Pan children. I remember singing it by candlelight as we promenaded around the Children's Dining Room. It also became a favorite lullaby for my grandchildren. It didn't matter if it was Christmastime or not, when my youngest grandson heard, *Wish You Merry Christmas...* he knew it was nap time.

During devotions in Peter Pan, we sang many, many Bible songs. *Away in a Manger, Jesus Loves Me, This Little Light of Mine,* and *Jacob's Ladder* were some of my favorites.

While I was in Peter Pan several college students were hired over the summer as playground helpers. These ladies were kind, pretty and fun. They played games with us such as Red Rover and Leap Frog. They also taught us some fun new songs, three of which I still remember: *The Soap Bubble Song, The Crocodile Song,* and Jeannie's favorite Peter Pan playground song: *In a Jelly Jelly Island But Ya Better Keep a Smilin' by the Sea.* We aren't sure those are the correct words and that's all we remember, but we've sure had a lot of fun singing this together over the years.

Girl Scouts sang all the time. I can still hear Mrs. Lane singing *Make New Friends,* and *When'er You Make a Promise.*

As teenagers in the Home, we listened to rock and roll on WING radio. Today, the 'oldies' bring back precious memories of singing those songs with my friends at the Home. It's fun for me to reminisce with many of the old songs, about where I was, what I was doing, or whom I was with at the time.

Elementary Christmas Program

I was in second grade and it was time for the Christmas pageant. I was cast as an angel. Children of all ages were gathered backstage; angels, shepherds, Mary, Joseph, wise men. We were trying so hard to be quiet and stand still, but we were so very excited and anxious to start the program. We had been practicing our parts for weeks. Let's get this show on the road!

Suddenly, everything came to a standstill. There was a medical emergency. The choir director had become ill, and an ambulance was called. As we all tried to catch a glimpse of the activity, we were herded even farther backstage.

The teacher who stepped up and took control of these angels, shepherds, and wise men was the third-grade teacher, Mrs. Bessie Peterson. Mrs. Peterson was a slight woman, not much taller than 5 feet. She seemed old to me, probably in her 40s, but maybe even her 50s. She would be my teacher the following year. Mrs. Peterson seemed to be worried about how she could keep all these youngsters under control and ready to go back on stage when the time was right. And she hit on the perfect solution. Christmas Carols! She would lead the children in singing songs. We were excited, too. What would we sing? *Away In a Manger? Jingle Bells? Frosty the Snowman?* We loved these songs.

But no, she led these little children, kindergartners, 1st, 2nd, and 3rd graders, her hands raised in as fine a fashion as any of the great maestros, in a rousing rendition of *Angels from the Realms of Glory.*

We all fell silent. Not one single child knew that song. Poor Mrs. Peterson was bewildered. She told us how disappointed she was, that everyone should know *Angels from the Realms of Glory.* I've never forgotten the sad feeling of having let her down.

And, I made it a point to learn *Angels from the Realms of Glory*, ready to sing it in any emergency situation that might arise from then on.

Easter

"Here comes Peter Cottontail." –Steve Nelson and Jack Rollins

Our Easter celebration at the Home started on Thursday evening with a Holy Communion service attended only by church members. Good Friday services were held on Friday evening and everyone living on main campus was required to attend.

On Saturday, an egg-decorating contest was held in each cottage. Children were each given a hard-boiled egg of their own to decorate any way they chose, with prizes awarded for the best decorated eggs in each cottage. We could then eat our eggs as a tasty treat. I remember participating in these contests only as a younger child, but I believe older children could still participate if they desired. The ladies from the American Legion Auxiliary hosted an Easter egg hunt each year for the Peter Pan children.

The dining room was always bright and colorful for Easter breakfast each year. Tables were decorated with a potted tulip or daffodil. We were greeted with an Easter basket and a balloon tied to each of our chairs. A special Easter breakfast menu was served: a half-grapefruit topped with a maraschino cherry, scrambled eggs with diced ham, and hot cross buns. Once we cleaned our plates, we could start eating our candy. The baskets and balloons were also provided by the American Legion Auxiliary. Members of this group filled the baskets with candy, and tied the balloon to each chair. These kind women then joined us children at breakfast, Chapel services, and Easter dinner.

Even before breakfast, we attended Sunrise Service at 6:30 a.m. The Chapel was beautifully adorned with purple, pink and white daffodils, narcissus, and tulips grown by Mr. Jackson in the Home's greenhouse.

Easter Chapel services were held at 10:30 a.m. During this service, students who had been attending Rev. Howard's confirmation class over the past year were baptized by sprinkling, and accepted into Church membership.

Easter dinner was served at noon. The menu was always about the same: ham served with either raisin, pineapple or cherry sauce, tossed salad, scalloped or sweet potatoes, a vegetable, homemade dinner rolls, and ice cream. Before we were dismissed, our guests from the American Legion Auxiliary presented each senior girl with a white zippered Bible, while each senior boy received a black Bible. I still have my Bible to this day.

The day before Easter was Loualtha's and Joe's first visit of the year, and a shopping trip was almost always on the agenda. Loualtha usually bought Jeannie and me a new Easter outfit. The boys bought something, too, but they didn't need any new Easter clothing since they wore their military uniforms as they marched in parade to Chapel.

Loualtha and Joe stayed overnight in Xenia and attended the Chapel service with us. Arrangements were made so we could sit with them in the back rows rather than with our cottage group. They took pictures of us and our friends all decked out in our Easter outfits before they left for home.

A special ritual each Easter for senior girls was the purchase of Easter outfits. Each girl was given $125.00 from the state to spend on clothing for not only Easter but for graduation and job interviews as well. We were all given a day off school to shop at local department stores. We were expected to purchase a suit, hat, purse, gloves, shoes and a coat. After purchasing a navy blue dress with a navy and white checkered coat, red purse and hat, white shoes and white gloves, I still had money left over to buy at least three more dresses and a second pair of shoes. I didn't think my new Easter outfit matched very well overall, but I liked the pieces individually. I fell in love with the red hat first, but I couldn't find an outfit that went well with it. I wouldn't give up on that hat, which was silly in retrospect, because I never wore it again after that Easter.

The younger girls on campus were provided with state-issued 'coordinates.' These cotton skirts with matching blouses came in several pastel shades: pink, blue, yellow, lavender, and green. The Peter Pan and junior campus girls wore dresses with fancy Easter bonnets that were passed down from year-to-year. Sometimes we made our own Easter bonnets using paper plates and crepe paper. The Peter Pan and junior campus boys wore suits that I imagine were passed down from year to year.

Memorial Day

"In Flanders Fields the poppies blow, between the crosses row on row
That mark our place; and in the sky, the larks, still bravely singing, fly
Scarce heard amid the guns below." –John McCrae

"It's too heavy, please help me," I implored the teenage girl who was walking with my group of little girls and boys. My flower basket was extremely heavy for my little arms, and I didn't think I could carry it much farther. And, for the umpteenth time, the kind helper caught up with me and carried my basket for a few short steps.

It was Memorial Day, one of the most solemn and celebrated days at the Home. The highlight of the day was the parade in which every Home child participated. We were all dressed in white. Each girl wore a white skirt, white blouse, and our black and white school shoes. The younger boys wore white pants and white shirts and their black shoes. We were lined up according to height, girls on one side and boys on the other, partners holding hands. We girls each carried a metal basket full of beautiful, sweet smelling peonies raised in our Home greenhouse. The baskets were made by high school boys in Metal Shop, each having a nail extending from the bottom of the basket so it could be placed in the ground. The younger boys each carried an American flag. The parade was led by our Home band, followed by the boys' military companies, and the girl's high school choir. The younger children followed, holding hands with their partner while carrying their flowers or flag with the other.

The parade proceeded very slowly to the beat of the band's mournful medley of *Nearer My God to Thee* and *Flee as a Bird to Your Mountain*. It wound its way around the parade field and around the chapel to the small, quiet cemetery where each eternally sleeping child would be remembered and honored.

Who were these children buried in our little cemetery? A diphtheria epidemic complicated with scarlet fever in 1889–90 resulted in 234 cases of diphtheria in the Home, with 35 children dying. Their nurse, Miss Olive

Memorial Day, 1957, Darlene and Jerry, as the Home's youngest children, led the parade. In approximately the tenth row, I'm the little girl who looks like she's begging for help. I was...those baskets were heavy!

Smith, refused to desert these young children. She also died and is buried in the Home cemetery with the children. Also laid to rest here in the little Home cemetery were several other children who passed away during their years in the Home, including two who drowned in the pond which once existed on the Home grounds.

Once the parade reached the cemetery, the children took their places beside the headstones marking each grave. *Flowers That Are Springing* was sung while the flowers and flags were placed beside the headstones at the appropriate places in the song.

A solemn ceremony followed with students reciting the Gettysburg Address, *In Flanders Fields*, and *America's Answer*. I was chosen to recite *In Flanders Fields* during both my sophomore and junior years. The girls' high school choir sang *Cover Them Over with Beautiful Flowers*. The service was concluded with a three-gun salute followed by the playing of *Taps* with *Echo Taps*. Our best trumpet players were selected to play, and both Rick and Jerry had this honor while in high school.

This celebration was repeated every year while I lived in the Home. Many former students still go back yearly to honor these children with a similar program. Over the past several years, the cemetery has become the final resting place for recent ex-pupils and employees of the Home.

Recently each gravestone was professionally refurbished. Former students and employees were given the opportunity to purchase bricks with their names and dates of residence or service to the Home. These bricks were incorporated into a beautiful brick walkway leading to a marble monument with a statue of a little girl carrying a basket of flowers and a little boy with his flag, just like we carried every year while in the Home. The front of the monument tells the story of our cemetery and our Home. This is our way of trying to assure that the children who are buried here are remembered, and that our Home and its children will never be forgotten. My siblings and I each purchased a brick with our name and the year we graduated.

Halloween

"There are witches in the air." –Kenneth David Whiteley/Raffi Cavoukian

Halloween was a fun, let-your-hair-down kind of day. While in Peter Pan, our supervisors planned our costumes. Once we moved to the main campus, we came up with our own costume ideas.

School ended early on Halloween afternoon so we could go to our cottage to get ready for the Halloween parade. The Home Band led the parade around the parade field as we marched in cottage groups, dressed in our most creative costumes. Money prizes ranging from $.25 to $1.00 were awarded for best costumes. All Peter Pan and junior campus children participated in the parade. As we aged, we tended to gradually shift to spectators. However, prizes were awarded for 11th and 12th graders, so a few older kids still participated.

Mommy Carmen came up with the most creative costume ideas, usually theme costumes for the whole cottage. She put a lot of thought and care into them. I don't remember our Pan 6 costumes, but while in Taylor B our costumes were the best. When we returned from school to get ready for the parade, Mommy Carmen had everything ready for us to put on. We never knew ahead of time what our costume might be. She did all this planning and preparation as a surprise for us.

One year we dressed as the Class of 1960, fifty years later. Our costumes were complete with old dresses for girls and old suits for boys. Mommy Carmen acquired shawls, canes, wigs, white gloves, glasses, hats, mustaches, and beards. On our backs, she pinned a sign with the name of the student we represented from the Class of 1960. I represented Nancy B. I thought this was a really great costume idea. The following June, Mommy Carmen took us to the graduation ceremony for the Class of 1960 to see these older kids we had pretended to be.

The next year, still in Taylor B, we were farmers. Mommy Carmen had acquired bib overalls for each of us girls in the cottage, as well as straw hats and a red bandana. Everyone was a different kind of farmer. Some carried eggs or a bucket of milk. I no longer remember all the kinds of farmers we represented, but I was a potato farmer and carried a pitchfork with potatoes at the end of the prongs.

The best farmer by far was Clara, who was going to be a pig farmer. Mommy Carmen told us she envisioned a sweet little piglet for Clara to lead in the parade. As we were putting on our costumes, one of the Home farmers dropped off what he considered to be a little piglet. In my mind it was a pretty big pig. Once in the basement where we were all getting dressed, the piggy promptly pooped all over the floor. And then it sat down and wouldn't budge. So no piggy in our parade. Mommy Carmen started laughing hysterically and we all joined in.

Clara ended up being a bird hunter farmer. She carried a toy rifle, and a real dead black bird. Clara later told me that the bird didn't smell so it must have been fresh or frozen. Poor Clara hated carrying that dead bird even though she was wearing gloves. It was a funny day, at least for most of us.

I'm pretty sure my Taylor B cottage won the 1st place prize for both years. Our costumes were just that awesome!

Halloween evening was celebrated in many different ways depending on the cottage and age. There was one treat, though, that we could always count

Halloween in Taylor B, dressed as the Class of 1960, fifty years later. I'm fifth from the left in the front row, wearing a plaid shawl.

on. No matter the age, cottage, or supervisor...we had donuts and apple cider. It was the perfect Halloween treat.

In the evening, we celebrated with parties either in our cottages where we played games and bobbed for apples, or in the Armory where we played Bingo for prizes. One year in Taylor B we had a dinner party in the cottage, served and hosted by a veterans' organization. After dinner we girls bobbed for apples and later joined our guests in singing some of our favorite songs.

High school students attended a Halloween carnival in the gym, sponsored by our teachers. We were each given a stack of tickets to use at the amusement-type games: dart throwing, fortune telling, basketball shooting, fish pond, bowling, cane rack, ball-in-the-can, cake walk, and dunking machine, all for little prizes such as stuffed animals, hats, and canes. The dunking machine was the most popular game. It was held at the swimming pool where we tried to dunk our principals into the water. My favorite game was the Cake Walk. Teachers and other employees from around the Home donated homemade cakes to be awarded as prizes for this game. The game was similar to musical chairs. We walked around a circle on the floor until the music stopped. One stop on the circle was designated as a cake winner. It was such a treat to win a whole cake to share with our friends...or not!

While Halloween was an especially fun day for me, I never went trick-or-treating while in the Home. I always wanted that experience, so on my first Halloween out of the Home, and shortly after my 19th birthday, I went trick-or-treating around my neighborhood. Just to say I did!

Thanksgiving

"All little children on Thanksgiving Day, bow their heads and quietly pray."
—A little prayer I learned in Kindergarten

Our celebration began with a Service of Thanksgiving in the Chapel. Following the service we were served a traditional dinner complete with turkey and dressing, mashed potatoes and gravy, cranberry sauce, vegetables, rolls, and pumpkin pie. The dining room was decorated with a large table at the front of the room, made festive with a cornucopia filled with fruit. Pilgrims, candles, and autumn décor completed the scene, and a fruit bowl adorned each table. After dinner, only seniors could leave with family for the long weekend. Picnic suppers with peanut butter and jelly sandwiches, potato chips, and an apple or orange were sent to each cottage for the evening meal so that kitchen employees could spend the rest of Thanksgiving Day with their families. The weekend was filled with open gyms, Orfenz Den gatherings, and basketball games.

Christmas

"Wish you Merry Christmas, Hark the Joyous Song...."
—Sara E. Collins, a Home Teacher

"It's Christmas, wake up everyone!" exclaimed Lucy, who slept in the little trundle bed next to mine.

Early Christmas morning in Peter Pan I could hear the soft sound of carolers winding their way through our cottages, the sound growing ever louder as they approached. The Home choir shuffled along singing the joyous melody of our very own *Home Christmas Carol*, waking up sleeping children as they passed through. This scene would be repeated every year I lived in Peter Pan. The carolers were comprised of the older choir students joined by a group of ex-pupils.

Christmas was the most special time of all at the Home. Many organizations including the Association of Ex-Pupils, veterans' organizations from around the state, employees of the Home, and even complete strangers pitched in to make sure we children always had a wonderful Christmas.

The campus was beautifully decorated. A large evergreen tree at the entrance gates, decorated with hundreds of colored lights, greeted visitors to the Home. Each lamppost hosted a red and white striped cane. The main building was decorated with colored lights that streamed from the tower to the porch, where a large wooden Santa stood next to a blinking Season's Greetings sign. Large cut-out figures from *The Peanuts Gang* adorned the band shell. To decorate the Peter Pan lawn, the boys in the Woodworking shop created a large wooden cut-out of Santa with his sleigh being pulled by reindeer. Each cottage received a real evergreen tree about a week before Christmas. We decorated our trees with a mix of store-bought and homemade decorations. Santas, snowmen, snowflakes, and mangers added to the magic. Excitement was in the air.

On Christmas Eve, each Peter Pan child was given a brand new pair of pajamas and slippers. As soon as supper was finished, we quickly changed into the pajamas because we knew that Santa would be stopping by each cottage to wish us a Merry Christmas and to give us a little gift, a preview of Christmas morning. Santa never let us down. He arrived with a bag full of toys, candy, and fruit—something for each child. When he left, we scampered off to bed in eager anticipation of Christmas morning, when we would be awakened by the beautiful carolers. Christmas morning always brought more presents and time to play with our new toys.

Once living on main campus, we awakened on Christmas morning and opened our presents before breakfast, although we didn't seem to have much time before eating to enjoy our new gifts. Christmas breakfast by candlelight was made even more special as our carolers entered the dining room, back from their journey through Peter Pan and the hospital. Each caroler held a lighted candle and slowly wound their way around the dining room, singing our *Home Christmas Carol*. The dining room was beautifully decorated with a 30-foot lighted tree, as well as several smaller, lighted trees placed around the room. Each table was decorated with evergreen branches and Christmas bulbs. So beautiful and so mystical.

Christmas morning was the one time we were permitted to visit all the other cottages. Girls could visit boys' cottages and vice versa. I loved seeing how each cottage was decorated. These cottage visits were made even more enjoyable because I could spend this time with my boyfriend. This was the perfect time to see his cottage and show him my cottage, to exchange Christmas gifts, and the best part of all...to steal a Christmas kiss, under the mistletoe or not.

Christmas dinner was next on the agenda. Roast beef, mashed potatoes and gravy, and Miss Lillian's dinner rolls were usually on the menu, followed by ice cream for dessert. The Home's roast beef and mashed potatoes were outstanding, and I think the gravy was the best gravy I've ever had. Miss Lillian's dinner rolls were just about everyone's favorite menu item.

After Christmas dinner, most children were permitted to leave, or as we called it, "go home" to spend a pre-approved Christmas break with family or friends, returning by supper time on New Year's Eve. My family was fortunate because, after the first year when we weren't yet allowed to leave with family, we always went to Loualtha and Joe's house to spend the holidays with them.

Some of the children had no family to visit and stayed at the Home over the holidays. My heart always hurt for those kids. It was hard to feel joy when my roommate, best friend, or boyfriend had to stay at the Home that week. The staff tried to make this time special for those children with outings and special treats. Various veterans' groups served holiday meals and gave these children extra presents. I always wondered if they had as much fun over the holidays as I had, or if they even had any fun at all.

Many of the children with families in the Cleveland area traveled by train to be met by their families. Early Christmas afternoon, Rev. Howard picked us up in the Home bus and drove us to the Dayton train station. We were each given a sack lunch to enjoy during our ride. I was always a little afraid standing on the platform as that huge New York Central train, huffing and puffing, pulled into the station. As a little girl, I would grab Rev. Howard's hand and hold onto it for dear life.

The train ride seemed to take forever as it traveled across the state. Many years the weather was bitterly cold and the train would be forced to stop and sit due to frozen locks or brakes. We younger Home kids had so much fun on those trips, running back and forth between the cars. The oldest Home student was put in charge of all of us. He didn't spoil our fun at all because he always slept the whole trip. One year the train derailed, causing a huge delay. Luckily no one was hurt, but it scared us. Rick always slept through the whole trip, holding onto a picture of his girlfriend as he snored away. He didn't even wake up when the train derailed, and we laughed as he grabbed that picture even tighter. We rode on the train all the way to the Terminal Tower station in Cleveland, where Loualtha and Joe would be waiting for us. After they gathered our belongings and we were settled in their car, they drove around downtown Cleveland to show us all the beautiful holiday lights. In later years the train ceased operations, and we rode the Greyhound Bus from Xenia to Akron. Rev. Howard always provided our transportation to the station and saw us off, and the kitchen staff always provided us with a sack lunch.

The morning after Christmas, Loualtha and Joe pretended that it was Christmas morning. Their tree was surrounded with presents which we eagerly opened. Friends and family stopped by to join us for breakfast and festivities. Loualtha always made her traditional Christmas breakfast of corned beef hash. We spent the rest of the holiday week visiting family and friends, playing indoor games, as well as playing outside in the snow.

On Sunday during the holiday weekend, we attended the family Christmas party potluck dinner with all our aunts, uncles, and cousins at the Odd Fellows Hall. Someone always picked up Mom and brought her to the party. We could count on Aunt Lenora to bring her cabbage, carrot, and pineapple jello salad. Old Uncle Ed always grabbed my knees—he did this to Jeannie and all my female cousins, too. Uncle Stanley sang his favorite song to us girls, *Oh She has Freckles on Her, But She's Pretty*. The men played pool. It looked like fun, but we children were not allowed to participate for fear we might scratch the felt on the table. The four of us participated in the family gift exchange by purchasing a small gift for each person at the party. And after dinner, my cousin Lauri joined Jeannie and me for a brisk walk around the block to make room in our tummies for dessert.

The week always passed by way too quickly, and it would be time to return to the Home before we knew it. Once back at the Home, it was time for the New Year's Eve celebrations. Children in 6th, 7th, and 8th grades celebrated with a game night in the gym. With music and snacks provided by Mr. Might, the high school students danced in the New Year, and celebrated with hugs and kisses at midnight. I'll never forget leaving the dance my senior year, January 1, 1969. As I walked out of the Den, it had just started snowing, big beautiful flakes that swirled like diamonds around us as we walked back to our cottages. I was carrying my brand new transistor radio. Our favorite station, WING, was playing a countdown of the greatest hits of 1968, and it was time to announce the #1 song for the year, *Windy* by the Association. My heart was full of joy as I listened to one of my favorite songs, realizing this was the beginning of my last year in the Home.

New Year's Day was the one day of the year when we could sleep in. Breakfasts put together by the dining staff had been delivered to our cottages the day before—little variety boxes of cereal, milk, and oranges. Such a treat for us!

After a lazy New Year's Day, it was back to school and back to the routine. The holidays were over.

The Children I Once Knew

Once was a day when I was nearly age one.
I was awakened by some noise, a road had begun.
"A HOME FOR THE ORPHANS!" the people did demand.
And in no time at all the first building would stand.
With a school and a chapel and playgrounds for play.
They grew cottages for children to come here and stay.
Young girls and young boys the ones of whom,
Were the first that I met, of the children I once knew.

Through years they would climb up my great trunk with charm.
While my branches would reach out to hold them from harm.
Each year they would march for soldiers who would die.
To come and to honor where young ones now lie.
In love some would walk holding hands with innocent grace.
In pride all would stand to make better this place.
With such strength and such promise the young ones all grew.
Oh how I long to be back with the children I once knew.

I remember spring concerts with music played so sweet.
And parades I did watch as they passed beneath my feet.
In summer they would swim in their own private lake.
In autumn they all gathered and my leaves they would rake.
Carols were sung, sled riding and snow fights.
While the ground was covered in a soft blanket of white.
Awakened by a whistle at morning's first dew.
To guide all day long, the children I once knew.

Unique for one purpose in truth all could tell.
That the Lord must have smiled when the first tree was fell.
Be it known to all who might come and to gaze.
That young girls and young boys came here to be raised.
Some cold some hungry this home they all were brought,
To live and be happy in this place that was wrought.
With each tear to each laughter my heart feels love true.
Oh the joy I remember, from the children I once knew.

—James E. Koski
Class of 1973
Used with Permission

This and That

"Appreciate the little things in life because one day you will look back and realize they were the big things." –Author Unknown

High School Class Projects. Starting in 9th grade, each class elected officers: President, Vice-President, Secretary, and Treasurer. Each class was assigned projects in order to earn money for class parties, class rings, and the prom. The president usually supervised these projects and assigned classmates to help as needed. Each student in the class paid dues to help build the coffers.

The Freshman Class collected newspapers and magazines for recycling. The Sophomore Class made money selling Christmas cards and candles. The items for sale sometimes changed over time.

The Junior Class paid for the Junior-Senior Prom as well as for more than half of the cost of class rings. Their need to make money was greater than the other classes. They sold candy, potato chips and gum to both children and employees. This class also managed the concession stand at all the Home football games as well as the concession stand in the Orfenz Den each weekend. In addition to what other classes did, my junior class also held a raffle to sell a Christmas fruitcake and a 5-pound box of chocolates. I laughingly wonder if we actually sold any fruitcake tickets!

We Home children loved our candy bars and bought them from the 'Candy Girl' when we could afford it. The most popular candy bars that I remember were: Milky Way, Mint Patties, Clark Bar, Powerhouse, Pay Day, Milk Duds, Sugar Daddy, Sugar Babies, Forever Yours, Bit-O-Honey, Three Musketeers, ZagNut, Baby Ruth and Heath bars.

My favorite brands of chewing gum from those days were Spearmint, Juicy Fruit, Doublemint, Dentyne, Dubble Bubble and Bazooka bubble gum.

Fire drills were held both in school and in our cottages several times a year. The cottage drills were held in what seemed to me to be in the middle of the night. No matter what the weather was, when the extremely loud alarm sounded, we all ran outside where we stood in our pajamas until everyone had been accounted for. I will always remember how cold it was on those dreadful winter nights.

Fire! The summer before I started 9th grade, the Main Building caught on fire. I believe workers were sandblasting and accidentally hit a bird's nest which caught on fire and ignited the building. The fire spread quickly, and many local fire departments were soon on the scene. They must have had a hard time extinguishing the fire because the flames seemed to last for hours. Finally, the fire department from Wright-Patterson Air Force Base arrived. They sprayed some kind of foam on the building, and the fire went out almost instantly.

We children sat and watched from a safe distance the whole time. I'll admit that in my fourteen-year-old mind, I was rooting for the fire. I didn't want the excitement to end. I gave no thought at all to the fact that the fire could easily spread to the nearby cottages or that someone could be hurt battling the flames. It was an exciting day for us orphans.

The back part of the Main Building was completely destroyed. I don't know what was lost in the fire. Luckily no one was hurt. A new annex was built the following year and included offices for the deans, the chaplain, social services, a lounge area, and a staff dining room.

In preparing the senior class for graduation, the senior girls were given the opportunity to participate in "Mrs. Prichard's Charm Course for Women." Mrs. Prichard offered this course free of charge to the senior girls at the Home. Her course covered poise, posture, hair styling, cosmetic techniques, wardrobe coordination, modeling techniques and etiquette. She taught us to walk properly by placing a book on our head and then walking up and down stairs. I remember having a hard time keeping my book in place as I walked. Several girls in my class met this challenge with beauty and grace, just like professional models.

Before graduating, each senior was given chest x-rays at the Xenia Public Health Clinic. Because I was planning to attend Nursing School, I needed several extra immunizations, some of which I received at the Home hospital and others at the Xenia Public Health Clinic.

During 12th grade, we seniors met with a psychologist hired by the Home to help prepare us for life after graduation. We met monthly in group therapy sessions where we discussed challenges we might face outside of the Home environment.

At the Home, there was a Home Advisory Committee (HAC). Although I was never a member of this group which consisted of two delegates from each grade, Jeannie was a member for each of her high school years. The HAC met regularly to address ideas for the betterment of the lives of the Home kids. During my high school years they were able to institute a Family Meal Night each Wednesday so families could eat together in the dining room. Even Peter Pan children were brought to the main dining room to eat with their older siblings.

The HAC served as escorts and gave tours to visitors of the Home. The Honor Roll students also helped to serve as escorts. I was never a member of the HAC, but loved being asked to escort our guests as an Honor Roll student. Our guests could be anyone, but they were usually members of various veterans' organizations or members of the state legislature.

Each year the Home students were invited to attend the Rotary Club Pancake Day at the Xenia Field House. The event ran all day long, so we were assigned to attend at breakfast, lunch or dinner. The menu was always the same and always delicious—pancakes, sausage, and orange juice. I think we all looked forward to Pancake Day.

'an old-fashioned orphan paper pick-up.'

During my high school years, a monthly Birthday Dinner program was initiated. Every child celebrating a birthday that month was invited to attend. This dinner was hosted by Superintendent Col. Stephan, and held in the Teachers' Dining Room. Miss Lillian, our favorite baker, provided a beautiful cake each month. Avon supplied gifts of sachets, nail polish, cologne, after shave, lotion, soap, and candles for the birthday children.

Each year the American Legion and its Auxiliary sponsored an Americanism Essay contest for students in the 10th, 11th, and 12th grades. A boy and a girl winner were announced from each grade in participating schools. I won this contest each of the three years. The reward was a trip to Columbus with other winners from all over the state. We toured the Statehouse and Capitol Building during the morning where the State Auditor, Secretary of State, or Lieutenant Governor spoke to our group in the Rotunda of the State House. We also sat in on a meeting in the Senate Chambers. The rest of the day was spent touring a different Columbus location each year. The locations I toured were the *Columbus Dispatch* newspaper, the Ohio State Highway Patrol Academy, and Lazarus department store. I particularly remember the Highway Patrol Academy where the beds were made so perfectly and tightly that we bounced dimes on the bedspreads. I was glad the Home wasn't so strict when we made our beds!

There was also an Association of Ex-Pupils Essay Contest. Each year this group of former students held an essay contest for high school students at the Home, selecting a different topic each year. Cash prizes were awarded for two winners in each grade, $2.50 for 1st place and $1.50 for 2nd place. I don't remember ever winning this contest.

I remember a fun visit to the Home from Smiley Burnette. He played Charlie Pratt, the engineer of the Hooterville Cannon Ball on *Petticoat Junction*, one of my favorite television shows at the time. He ate dinner with us children in the dining room and talked about the show. He was the first movie star I ever saw in person.

The Home owned two green sixty-seat buses that were used for off-campus adventures such as sporting events, band trips, Christmas shopping, and trips back and forth to Camp Cooper.

The Home grounds were always beautifully manicured, nicely mowed, and there was no paper anywhere to be seen! There was no better way to pick-up paper and trash than what I like to call 'an old-fashioned orphan paper pick-up.' Once or twice a month during good weather, girls (the boys did this on their side of campus, too) formed a long row and walked the campus, picking up any paper or trash along our way. It didn't take long at all, and the results were amazing. I was awfully proud of our beautiful campus.

The summer before my senior year, I was chosen to attend Buckeye Girls' State. The American Legion Auxiliary sponsored this annual week-long event held at Capital University in Columbus. My friend Joanne was the other delegate from the Home. Two boys in my class were chosen to attend Buckeye Boys' State, held at Ohio Northern University in Ada. At Buckeye Girls' State I was assigned to the mythical city of Janis. In order to learn more about our government, we campaigned and held elections for government positions anywhere from the city level to the governor of the state. I ran unsuccessfully for state senator in the general election. One of the girls in my dorm ran unsuccessfully for governor, and all the girls in our dorm joined her political party and her ballot as we supported her candidacy. We all went down together, and then had to scramble to get any kind of job in our city. I believe I ended up as Police Commissioner. In spite of losing my bid for senator, it was a great experience.

The Vietnam War was in full swing during my high school years. Many of the Home boys graduated, went straight into the military and on to Vietnam. This was a worrisome time for all of us. I didn't know the two older boys from the Home who died serving our country in Vietnam. After I graduated, I kept in touch with my friend Donnie who had left the Home two years before me. While he was in Vietnam, my Aunt Loualtha and I sent care packages to him. He specifically requested chocolate chip cookies, and condiments to make his meals taste better. We sent homemade cookies along with a box full of packets of salt and pepper, mustard and ketchup. Thankfully, Donnie made it home safely.

As a senior at Christmastime, I joined a group of volunteers at the Red Cross in Xenia. We helped families of active Vietnam service members make tape recorded messages to send to their loved ones overseas. My assignment was to set up the tape recorder so the family members just had to press "Play." We then left the room to allow them privacy as they recorded their messages. Other volunteers were responsible for mailing the tapes to the proper locations. These wives, mothers and fathers, brothers, sisters and children seemed grateful for the opportunity to be able to send this gift to their service member. Many left in tears. I was extraordinarily proud to be able to help our servicemen receive this token of Christmas cheer.

The summer between 10th and 11th grade, Irene and I were chosen to represent Woodrow Wilson High School at an annual five-day Red Cross Leadership Camp at Camp Cricket Holler near Dayton. We attended workshops and participated in discussions to promote leadership qualities in high school students. We each stayed with a different family in Dayton for the week. I stayed with Mrs. Curry and her daughter, Laura. We rode a city bus to camp each day with Laura teaching me how to navigate the bus system. One day, Laura couldn't attend camp, and I was proud to be able to figure out how to take the bus by myself.

Each evening Laura's boyfriend and his friend Gary came over to visit. Gary's aunt and uncle had both been raised in the Home so they all knew about it. We four became good friends. The two boys took Laura and me out for donuts before they went home...every single night. Cars, donuts, boys. I don't remember much about the camp, but I'll never forget being able to be a 'real' teenager for a week. Laura and I stayed in touch for a year or two after this adventure.

Col. Stephan, the Home superintendent, was the legal guardian of all the Home children, and he remained our guardian until we each reached twenty-one years old or got married. I was twenty when I got married—it was quite common to marry at twenty years of age back then. I needed to obtain not only Col. Stephan's blessing, but also his legal permission to wed.

My fiancé and I made an appointment with Col. Stephan, and he interviewed both of us. Col. Stephan was cute as he acted as if he were my father. He wanted to know all about my fiancé. How did I meet him? How long had I known him? Was he a good guy? Where did he work? Did he make a decent living? Would I work? Where would we live? Would we have children right away? He then discussed both the blessings and pitfalls of marriage. I felt his concern and maybe even a sort of fatherly love. We then rode downtown together to the Greene County Courthouse where Col. Stephan relinquished his custody over me, and I was free to get married.

Graduation Day

"Oh the future lies before me...." –Armen

Whenever I hear that old familiar tune, *Pomp and Circumstance*, my eyes start to tear up, and it's Graduation Day again for me, the most bittersweet day of all in the Home. The seniors are graduating and leaving the Home, moving on to start brand new lives. Everyone else is there to watch, say good-bye, and be left behind. Graduation Day was a big deal at the Home.

I was fourteen, just finishing 8th grade, when Rick graduated. It was the first graduation I attended where I actually knew someone graduating. Although Rick and I weren't really close back then, I still felt the painful sting of separating from a sibling. Rick started his graduation day by wearing shorts to

Rick, the graduate, 1965.

the dining room at breakfast. His best buddy joined in this rebellion against a long-standing rule of always wearing long pants to the dining room. Mere hours before they would leave the Home, they were placed on 'detention' for the remainder of the day, not really a punishment at all. The rest of the kids in the dining room cheered them on. I was so proud of my big brother—he beat the system!

The Baccalaureate service was held that morning during Chapel. The graduating seniors filed into the Chapel wearing their caps and gowns, boys in dark blue and girls in white. The Commencement ceremony began promptly at 1:00 p.m. at the band shell. Family and friends from outside of the Home, as well as most other Home students attended, filling the viewing area to capacity. Almost every one of my relatives, my mother, aunts, uncles, and cousins came to Rick's graduation. We all sat on dark green, freshly painted metal seats. Unfortunately, some of the paint wasn't dry. At least one of my aunts ended up with green paint all over the back of her dress. That wet green paint was the topic of family gatherings for many years after.

Jeannie graduated two years later, and I was really sad. She had always been my rock, my big sister. Again all the relatives came for graduation day. Jeannie was beautiful in her cap and gown. I cried a lot that day.

My own graduation was two years after Jeannie left. While I didn't wear shorts to the dining room, I did exercise my own little rebellion. I usually walked the straight and narrow, but I knew that many of the other kids sneaked out at night. Some got caught and were placed on detention, while others got away with it. Sneaking out at night was like earning a badge of honor, and I decided I didn't want to leave the Home without trying it at

Jeannie, the graduate, 1967. My mother, Bernice, is behind Jeannie's right shoulder in the striped dress. My Aunt Beulah is behind Jeannie's left shoulder. My cousin, Irene, is far right with her back to the camera. Aunt Ruthie is beside her.

Janice, the graduate, 1969.

least once. So I made plans to sneak out after Prom on my last night, to meet some friends and hang out for a while...just to say I did it. My roommate Kathy helped me get past our supervisor and out of the cottage. She stayed awake to help me sneak back in. I was scared. I had always been a good girl, and I certainly didn't want a bad mark on my record the last day. I didn't go far, just across the street to behind the Vocational Building where I met a few friends, both girls and guys. We talked for a while and said our goodbyes, as we knew we were all leaving the next day. Then we hurried back to our cottages and our beds. Good ol' Kathy was right there to let me back in. And I did it! I could now say I had sneaked out.

Richard M. Nixon was the President of the United States the year I graduated. I thought it would be fun to invite him to my graduation. With thoughts of how special we orphans were and how exciting his presence would be for all of us, I mailed off an invitation to him at the White House, hoping that just maybe we were exceptional enough for him to drop everything and attend. Of course he didn't show up, but I did receive a nice, formally printed congratulatory note from him and the First Lady, Pat Nixon. This note is still in my box of Home treasures.

My Graduation Day began with the Baccalaureate Service at 10:30 a.m. I wore my new graduation dress. Short dresses were in style back then, and I bought the shortest dress I have ever worn in my life. It was cute, white with bell sleeves, and did I mention short? Oh my! But with my cap and gown, no one could tell.

Father Erwin J. Bertke, the priest at St. Brigid Catholic Church in Xenia gave the address. It felt so strange to finally be wearing my cap and gown and filing into the Chapel. So many emotions were swirling around inside me. I

Jerry, the graduate, 1970.

never thought this day would ever actually happen for me. Instead, I felt that I would be in the Home for the rest of my life. But here I was, excited to start a new chapter of my life, scared to leave the place that had been my home for the last thirteen years, sad to leave my friends and classmates, but most of all—sad to leave my little brother Jerry at the Home by himself.

I don't really remember my last lunch at the Home, but I'm sure I joined my cottage group in the dining room. I'm certain we had a wonderful final Sunday dinner, complete with Miss Lillian's dinner rolls, and ice cream for dessert, just the same as every other Sunday during my thirteen-year stay at the Home. But I don't remember any of it. In my excitement it all seemed to pass in a blur.

My Commencement Service began promptly at 1:00 p.m. at the Band Shell. The Home was 100 years old that year, 1969, and we had the honor of being the 100th graduating class. Judge Raymond E. Shannon of the Court of Appeals in Cincinnati delivered our Commencement address. In addition to my diploma, I was awarded a $100 scholarship from the American Legion to use for nursing school. I also received the Girl Citizenship Award, a medal and $25. And then the thought crossed my mind—I had sneaked out last night! What if I had been caught?

After the ceremony my mother, brothers, sister, baby nephews, aunts, uncles and cousins surrounded me with hugs, congratulations, gifts and lots of pictures. We seniors had to be gone, off the Home grounds by 5:00 pm.

But my business at the Home wasn't finished. Social Services was holding money, $40 in my case, for each senior to pick up. Before we could receive our money, we had to empty our room, clean it, have it inspected and signed off by our supervisor. I didn't ask and still don't know the exact source of that money. Was this money held for me after cleaning houses on the weekends? Did it come from money the state paid for my institutional care? I highly doubt that it was child support paid by my father as he was out of the picture for the most part.

My family helped load all my belongings into their cars, and I cleaned my room like a madwoman. I finished, signed off, hugged Mrs. Quickle goodbye one last time, collected my money and was finally ready to go. Saying goodbye to Jerry and leaving him there by himself was hard for me. Although I knew I would see him again soon and he would be graduating the following year, it was still rough to leave him behind.

4,674 days; twelve years, nine months and fifteen days; and now it was over. I cried that day so long ago when I arrived at the Home, but I cried so much harder when, almost thirteen years later, I left the Home forever. At the Baccalaureate Service that morning, the choir had sung *The Future* by Armen. It had never rung so true for me as it did that day. *Oh I often sit and wonder, when the sun is sinking low, where shall yonder future find me? Does but God in Heaven know?*

Finding My Way

"A person often meets his destiny on the road he took to avoid it." –Jean de La Fontaine

From the time I was a little girl, I knew I wanted to be a nurse. I read every one of the books in the Cherry Ames, Student Nurse series, and imagined I was right there with her in nursing school. During my time in the Home, some of my favorite employees were the nurses. I loved to talk with them about nursing whenever I got the chance.

I was so frustrated when our vocational principal rejected my request to help out in our hospital and thus prepare myself for my chosen profession. Despite the skills I learned in my Commercial classes, I believed that I would never make use of them because I would be a nurse.

I knew I would need credits in both algebra and chemistry if I wanted to attend a nursing school. Because our high school was small, we had only one higher math class, Set Theory, which combined algebra, geometry and trigonometry. Since I had done well in previous math classes, I signed up. As I have mentioned, I struggled in this class. Four of the brightest students to ever graduate from the Home were also in this class. Mrs. Lane, the math teacher, worked well with these bright students; together they seemed to enjoy the class and have great discussions. Mrs. Lane even let those boys take the homework answer book back to their cottage to work together in the evenings to solve math problems. The only other girl in the class seemed as lost as I was. Mrs. Lane would encourage us to ask questions, but I was so lost that

I didn't even know what to ask. I ended up with a C, but never believed I learned much in that class.

Mrs. Lane was also the chemistry teacher. She knew my math background and knew that I'd struggle in chemistry class. She also knew I needed a credit in chemistry to get into nursing school, so she made a deal with me: if I turned in every homework assignment and turned in documentation for every experiment, she would pass me with a C regardless of my performance. My lab partner was one of those four smarties I mentioned earlier. He performed each experiment as I took notes and typed our papers. Mrs. Lane was true to her word: I received a C, but I knew I really didn't learn much about chemistry.

As my senior year was beginning, I had taken two English classes and three years of journalism. All the nursing schools I was considering required I take one more English class.

I approached our principal, "I need one more English credit to be accepted into nursing school. I'd like to take the senior English class this year to meet that requirement."

In the one and only senior English class that was offered, only boys were presently enrolled. It was touted as a college prep class, and seemed to be exactly what I needed to fulfill the requirements of these nursing schools.

"Oh no, I can't allow that," answered the principal. "You know that class is only for boys, and the only reason you want to take it is to be around the boys."

I showed him the catalogues from the schools and begged him, insisting I really needed this class, but he wouldn't budge. I never understood why only boys were permitted to take senior English. I ended up taking a fourth year of journalism. Though I loved journalism and writing, loved my teacher, made good grades, and spent a lot of time with Jerry in this class, I felt that this was not the class I needed.

During my senior year Rev. Howard took me on several nursing school visits, and I was drawn to a school in Columbus. At about the same time, our new guidance counselor took me to visit a hospital in his hometown of Gallipolis where his wife had gone to nurses training. Though I enjoyed the visit and found the hospital interesting, I didn't have the same warm feelings about this school that I felt for the Columbus school.

I took the National League for Nursing Exam. The guidance counselor said that my math grades "didn't set the world on fire," but I had passed. He strongly encouraged me to apply to the Holzer Hospital School of Nursing in Gallipolis, convincing me that I might not fit in the larger Columbus school. I followed his advice, applied, and was accepted. But, according to my acceptance letter, I needed an algebra class or at least to be tutored in algebra before I started classes the following September.

Algebra was not offered at that time because it was included in "Set Theory." I was reluctant to approach Mrs. Lane again, so I borrowed one of the old-fashioned algebra books still in her closet without her permission. I planned to tutor myself during the summer after graduation. However, as it turned out, I didn't spend much time studying that summer.

While writing my story, I did not realize or intend to make it seem as though girls were treated so much differently from boys in the Home. Those differences in opportunities now seem to jump off the pages at me. I know that in most cases this was just normal life in the 1960s. Gender equity has certainly come a long way since then.

After graduation, I moved to Barberton to live with Loualtha and Joe. With the money I saved that summer from working as a switchboard operator at Babcock & Wilcox, a scholarship from the American Legion and grants and loans from the nursing school, I would be financially able to complete the first year in the program. So I was off to nursing school....

In September, Loualtha and Joe dropped me off in Gallipolis. During orientation weekend, several traditional welcoming activities were held, one that was particularly bothersome to me. Each new student was given a baby bonnet, bib and pacifier. Wearing our baby attire, we were escorted at dark around the block where the hospital was located, each of us carrying a lighted candle. Tradition says that if the candle goes out during the walk, the offending student will flunk out and not make it to the capping ceremony. My candle was the only one that didn't stay lit. The older students were quick to assure me that this was a silly superstition and it didn't mean a thing, but there it was.

I shared a room with three other girls, all locals who went home every weekend. Those weekends exacerbated the loneliness and uncertainty that I was feeling. With no access to freeways at the time, it was a five-hour drive from Barberton and thus too far away for easy trips home. I was still missing the Home and my friends. After living with Loualtha and Joe for three months, I was miserable leaving them, too.

I wondered, "What have I done?"

I started to feel that this wasn't the place for me at all. I didn't want to flunk out, but I knew that my chemistry, algebra and English skills weren't adequate. And...my candle had gone out. Was it a sign? And the homesickness and the loneliness... I was done. Leaving all my belongings behind, I walked to the Greyhound bus station, bought a ticket and went home. When my aunt later drove me back to get my things, I met with the nursing school director, a sweet older lady whose main concern was how I would be able to support myself without a nursing degree. I told her I would be fine; I would be a secretary!

Since that time, I have had an interesting and successful secretarial career that included:

- Seven years as Secretary to the Wadsworth Chief of Police.
- Twelve years as Engineering Secretary at Goodyear Aerospace/Lockheed Martin.
- Eleven years as Part-time Recording Secretary for the Wadsworth Planning Commission.
- Fifteen years as Executive Assistant to the Senior Vice President at George Mason University, my last job before retirement.

I retired several years ago and moved back home to Wadsworth, Ohio, to enjoy my grandchildren and family. Despite being proud of my career, I remain a little disappointed in myself for not following through with my nursing dream. But I know in my heart that if I could go back to that day, and talk to that girl who got on the Greyhound bus to return home, I would still tell her to do the same thing. I'm content with the choices I've made.

50 Years Later

"Time flies over us, but leaves its shadow behind."
—Nathaniel Hawthorne

In June of 2019, I will celebrate the 50th anniversary of my high school graduation and my departure from the Home. I was in 9th or 10th grade on that Saturday morning, when a powerful feeling washed over me: "This is all there will be to my life. I will never leave this place." I truly believed it at the time. Now I can hardly believe that fifty years have already flown by since I left the Home and went out into the world, proving that long-ago teenager wrong.

In the first months after leaving, I was overwhelmingly sad. I missed my friends, my routine, and the life I knew. That void was filled mostly by spending time with Jeannie and my baby nephew. My orphan friends Joanne and Phyllis visited occasionally, and I spent weekends with them whenever I could. After I married, my husband and I visited Kathy and Cliff often, and even vacationed with them several times. But we all eventually got busy with our lives, our families and careers. I even stopped going to Reunions.

Several years ago one of my childhood friends from Peter Pan wrote and published her book about growing up in the Home. While we share many of the same memories, my sense of our childhood is still quite different from hers. I began to see how differently each of us Home kids remembers things. And as my memories started to flood back while reading her story, I knew in my heart that I needed to write my own.

I also discovered a need to find Mommy Carmen if I could. I had memories that I felt I needed to settle about her. I had no idea if she were still living, but because she had often spoken of her hometown, I had an idea of where to start looking. I did find her, and since then we have stayed in touch. As of this writing, she is ninety-three years old with her memory as sharp as ever.

Mommy Carmen and I have discussed our days together in Peter Pan and Taylor B. She remembers my black and blue spanking and some of my other memories the same way I do. She has apologized profusely, and said she was sorry that I have carried these memories into my adult life. Mommy Carmen begged me to try to remember only the good times we had together. We now exchange birthday and Christmas cards, and on my birthday each year she calls and sings "Happy Birthday" to me. I'm not sure if I have truly forgiven her, but I have made peace with Mommy Carmen.

Several years ago when I started attending annual AXP reunions again, I ran into Darlene, another "lifer" orphan. She was a year behind me in school, and we had been friends while in the Home. We renewed our friendship, and she encouraged me to return each year. Since then I've tried to make attending Reunion a priority. With the development of several Facebook sites established for ex-pupils, it is now easy to stay in contact with many of the kids I grew up with so long ago. I'm happy to say that I am now in touch with old friends from all across the country whom I thought I would never hear from again. And it has been an added blessing every year to meet ex-pupils who were in the Home before or after my time. It has been inspiring to spend time sharing and comparing memories from our different eras.

Good and bad, we each have our own memories of the time we spent at the Ohio Soldiers' and Sailors' Orphans' Home or the Ohio Veterans' Children's Home. We all just called it "the Home."

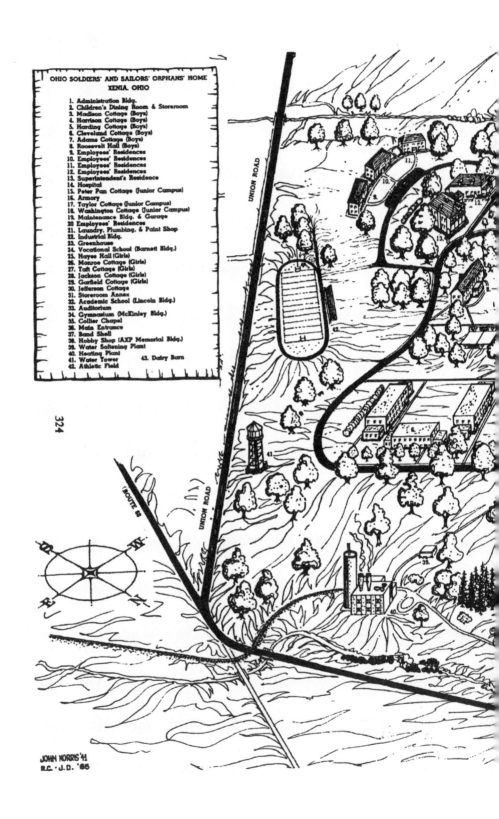

OHIO SOLDIERS' AND SAILORS' ORPHANS' HOME
XENIA, OHIO

1. Administration Bldg.
2. Children's Dining Room & Storeroom
3. Madison Cottage (Boys)
4. Harrison Cottage (Boys)
5. Harding Cottage (Boys)
6. Cleveland Cottage (Boys)
7. Adams Cottage (Boys)
8. Roosevelt Hall (Boys)
9. Employees' Residences
10. Employees' Residences
11. Employees' Residences
12. Employees' Residences
13. Superintendent's Residence
14. Hospital
15. Peter Pan Cottage (Junior Campus)
16. Armory
17. Taylor Cottage (Junior Campus)
18. Washington Cottage (Junior Campus)
19. Maintenance Bldg. & Garage
20. Employees' Residences
21. Laundry, Plumbing, & Paint Shop
22. Industrial Bldg.
23. Greenhouse
24. Vocational School (Barnett Bldg.)
25. Hayes Hall (Girls)
26. Monroe Cottage (Girls)
27. Taft Cottage (Girls)
28. Jackson Cottage (Girls)
29. Garfield Cottage (Girls)
30. Jefferson Cottage
31. Storeroom Annex
32. Academic School (Lincoln Bldg.)
33. Auditorium
34. Gymnasium (McKinley Bldg.)
35. Collier Chapel
36. Main Entrance
37. Band Shell
38. Hobby Shop (AXP Memorial Bldg.)
39. Water Softening Plant
40. Heating Plant
41. Water Tower
42. Athletic Field
43. Dairy Barn

324

JOHN NORRIS '41
R.C. · J.D. '65

We Called It The Home

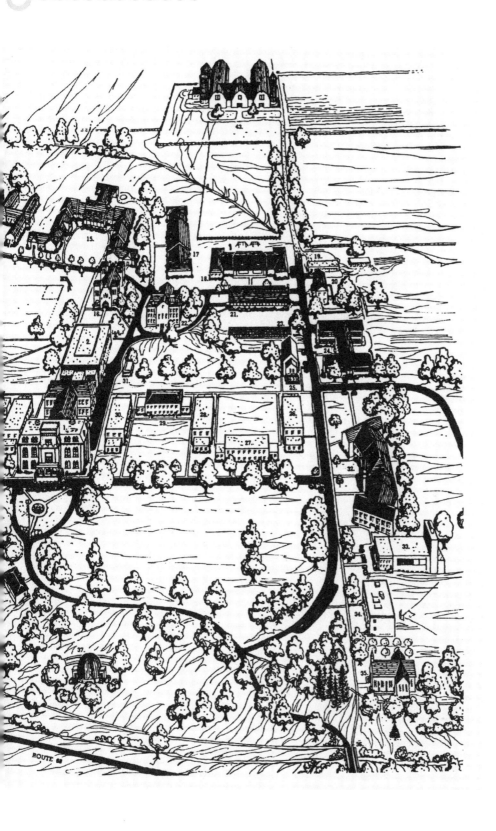

Notes

Books and publications which were helpful resources in the publication of *We Called it the Home*:

A Home of Their Own: The Story of Ohio's Greatest Orphanage (The Rooney Trust Fund, 2010) by Edward Lentz.

The Pride of Ohio: The History of the Ohio Soldiers' and Sailors' Orphans' Home at Xenia, Ohio 1868–1963 (Xenia: AXP, 1963) by Edward Wakefield Hughes and William Clyde McCracken with later editorial assistance by a number of other people associated with the Home.

The Home Review: Ohio Soldiers and Sailors Orphans Home, Xenia, Ohio. (Years reviewed: 1956-1969). Published monthly except July, August and September by the Home students.

Book Club Study Questions

1. Mommy Carmen
   a. Overall, do you believe Mommy Carmen was a more positive or negative influence in the little girls' lives? Give examples.

   b. Considering her role as their "mommy," and the time in history, was it acceptable for her to share her faith to the extent she did?

   c. Do you believe Mommy Carmen would be hired for her role as house mother if the Home existed today? Why or why not?

2. In so many ways this is a Rite-of-Passage story. Give examples of Janice learning lessons that help her move toward adulthood.

3. What is your reaction toward the scene in which Janice permanently loses her dating card? Was the Dean justified?

4. Janice's favorite person on campus was Reverend Howard. What did he do to earn her admiration?

5. Why do you think music was so important at the Home and in Janice's own life?

6. Loualtha and Joe
   a. How would you describe the role Loualtha and Joe play in Janice and her siblings' lives?

   b. Loualtha said she would find a way to keep the children together. Do you believe the Home was the best possible circumstance to make that happen at that time? Explain.

c. When the family sends the children to the Home, Loualtha reminds them they are all each other has and charges the older children to take care of the younger children. Give examples of the children trying to remain a family.

d. Did the Home try to keep the children together as a family? Why do you think they handled things as they did?

7. When Janice is home with her family she is delighted to be part of "Hen" parties, because this allows her to be included in adult talk. How important do you feel this is for children? What does it accomplish?

8. Ironically, Janice and her siblings return home for their first visit to the family just following their grandmother's death. Loualtha chooses to protect them from the funeral so they will remember Grandma "the way she was." This sets up years of confusion for Janice. How do you feel it is best to teach children about death?

9. What was your overall opinion of the Home?

a. What were the best things about it in the years Janice was there?

b. What were the worst things in those years?

10. Compare life at the OSSO Home when Janice grew up there with what you know of the foster system today. After reading this book, which seems better? Why?

11. Would the OSSO Home be a workable alternative today? Explain.

About the Author

Rick, Janice (center), and Jeannie.

After retiring from George Mason University in Fairfax, Virginia, Janice and her husband Jim moved back to Wadsworth, Ohio, to be closer to family.

Janice is a wife, mom to three awesome young adults, stepmother to another three awesome young adults, and mother-in-law to three more awesome young adults. She is Grandma to a plethora of very special young people; little sister to Rick and Jeannie; friend and sister-in-law to eight; and auntie to almost too many nieces and nephews to count.

She's an experienced secretary, friend, chef, grocery shopper, domestic engineer, pianist, seamstress, crochet freak, boo-boo kisser, family psychologist, chauffeur, matriculated orphan, and now an author.

While spending time with family is her priority, Janice also enjoys reading, writing, and crocheting. This memoir is her first book.